Palgrave Studies in Financial Services Technology

Series Editor
Bernardo Nicoletti, Rome, Roma, Italy

The Palgrave Studies in Financial Services Technology series features original research from leading and emerging scholars on contemporary issues and developments in financial services technology. Falling into 4 broad categories: channels, payments, credit, and governance; topics covered include payments, mobile payments, trading and foreign transactions, big data, risk, compliance, and business intelligence to support consumer and commercial financial services. Covering all topics within the life cycle of financial services, from channels to risk management, from security to advanced applications, from information systems to automation, the series also covers the full range of sectors: retail banking, private banking, corporate banking, custody and brokerage, wholesale banking, and insurance companies. Titles within the series will be of value to both academics and those working in the management of financial services.

Augusto Schianchi · Andrea Mantovi

The Economics of Cryptocurrencies and Digital Money

A Monetary Framework with a Game Theory Approach

palgrave
macmillan

Augusto Schianchi
Facoltà di Economia
Università di Parma
Parma, Italy

Andrea Mantovi
Facoltà di Economia
Università di Parma
Parma, Italy

ISSN 2662-5083 ISSN 2662-5091 (electronic)
Palgrave Studies in Financial Services Technology
ISBN 978-3-031-44247-6 ISBN 978-3-031-44248-3 (eBook)
https://doi.org/10.1007/978-3-031-44248-3

This Palgrave Macmillan imprint is published by the registered company Springer Nature Switzerland AG
The registered company address is: Gewerbestrasse 11, 6330 Cham, Switzerland

Paper in this product is recyclable.

Preface

In 2022 the price of major cryptocurrencies has been subject to large fluctuations, resulting in huge losses at the turn of the year. Intermediaries of crypto have displayed severe stress, and a number have gone broke, with the crack of FTX in November certifying the Minsky moment. In the words of The Economist, it has been dealt a catastrophic blow to the crypto's reputation and aspirations. Still, this is not the end.

The crypto revolution initiated by Bitcoin has generated tremendous enthusiasm. On the one hand, the advocates of decentralized consensus have been arguing about the relevance of getting rid of the "power" of central monetary institutions. On the other hand, the explosive market capitalization of Bitcoin and altcoins has stimulated the abrupt emergence of a network of exchanges of crypto assets. The crypto downfall of 2022 has definitely calmed the euphoria, and this is an ideal moment to take stock of events and refine judgments and prospects. The downfall, in our view, should not be considered an empirical rejection of the ambitions of Decentralized Finance (DeFi). At the time of writing investigations are under way, but evidence seems to witness that the downfall has been to a significant extent a crisis of crypto as *collateral*, a practice that can hardly be imputed to the philosophy of decentralized consensus.

The economics of crypto and new digital money is in rapid development. The revolution of decentralized consensus ignited by Nakamoto is characterized by the computer science of blockchain, still, on economic grounds, one is primarily interested in the interplay of the incentives that shape the objectives and the strategies of players. Game theoretic methods have taken the lead in shaping economic research on the subject. Along these lines we shall pursue a unifying view on the new forms of digital money, in conjunction with recent advances in monetary economics shaped by the principle of "no questions asked" (NQA). As a preliminary glimpse of our discussion, one may say that game theory distills the properties of the strategic equilibrium shaped by a blockchain protocol (section 1.2), and the principle of NQA (section 2.2) clusters the inherent monetary problems raised by new digital tokens as means of exchange and stores of value traded on a network of intermediaries. Around these conceptual pillars, one can frame both the theoretical inquiries on the strategic forces at play in the monetary arena and the policy debates on the design and regulation of new tokens.

The specific traits of the private production of new digital money pivot what these instruments can be expected to represent in the decades to come. Cryptocurrencies have displayed fluctuating values relative to standard currencies; therefore, with a more conservative attitude, stablecoins have been conceived so as to maintain (hopefully) stable value with respect to a widely accepted currency like the US dollar. This new form of privately produced money is attracting substantial interest; from an academic point of view, the crucial point is to discriminate its genuinely novel features (if any) from its inherent monetary status. In turn, central banks are exploring the possibility space for their own digital currencies to represent a centralized incarnation of digital money that the financial sector may accommodate in order to exploit recent technological advances without challenging the overall stability and relative allocation of resources among sectors. The feasibility of these scenarios is currently scrutinized with due care, witness the prudence with which many central banks are embarking on digital currency programming.

This short monograph is meant to address a manifold audience, encompassing students and researchers in economics and finance, professionals, sophisticated readers, and investors interested in the current evolution of money. In order to deal properly with such heterogeneity, we shall accompany analytical arguments and results with thorough comments meant to be useful not only for the least mathematically oriented reader. Recall, economic models are meant to straighten arguments and facilitate communication, and their relevance lies in their interpretation, not in the sophistication of equations. This is well-accepted economics. Not as well accepted may be the balance sheet representation of the monetary environment that some refer to as the ***hierarchy of money***. We shall rely on this truly compelling map of the monetary arena in order to frame our theoretical arguments. Time and again one hears that theorists inhabit an ideal heaven that is far too distant from reality. With the opposite attitude, it has been stated that, without a theory, reality does not even exist. Everyone is free to strike a position between these extremes. In what follows we shall strike our own position in terms of, hopefully, clear lines of reasoning.

New tokens should fit a financial environment that has changed after the unconventional monetary policies of recent years. Policymakers have entered uncharted territory with the combined policies of quantitative easing and interest rates at the lower bound. The sources and uses of liquidity have been reshuffled, and the size of the balance sheet of major central banks has increased by almost one order of magnitude. Furthermore, financial regulations introduced after the crisis of 2007–2009 have progressively displayed their bite. Charting the new environment is still an ongoing subject. Part of the new chart pertains to the marginal cost of enlarging the balance sheet of banks and non-banks. This marginal cost has been acknowledged as crucial for the feasibility of adjusting positions, posing, among other things, limits to arbitrage strategies.

In turn, monetary economics is undergoing a phase transition. The classical foundational notions that feature in standard manuals do not seem to exhaust the conceptual toolkit that researchers are currently operating. Over the last decade, the microstructure of financial markets has been refocused as a pivotal perspective for appreciating the riskiness and sustainability of positions and counterparty arrangements, and collateral flows have definitely entered the set of relevant monetary degrees of freedom.

Macroeconomics is undergoing a profound rethinking. Lord Adair Turner challenges the "mythological" vision of the banking sector that features in standard macroeconomic manuals. One reads that banks take deposits and channel these funds to borrowers, with a neutral attitude concerning the allocation of resources across sectors. Reality is another thing. Banks produce money and purchasing power, they are not simply matching savers and borrowers; the notorious $I = S$ relation is in dispute. In addition, banks have a selective attitude toward sectors; for instance, at the turn of the millennium banks were disproportionally financing ownership of real estate. More generally, according to Joseph Stiglitz, a poor account of the functioning of financial markets is one of the places where modern macroeconomics went wrong.

It is this challenging conceptual arena that our discussion is meant to fit in. We shall follow the BIS in looking at new tokens as new entries of the future monetary system. Chapter 1 introduces our methodological stance. Chapter 2 provides an overview of the economics of blockchain protocols, as well as our monetary perspective on the role of new tokens. Chapter 3 develops the foundational game theoretic representation of Proof-of-Work, which we enlarge in Chapter 4 by discussing more articulated models. Chapter 5 deals with stablecoins and central bank digital currency in the context of the future monetary system. Chapter 6 sketches the principles of regulation. Conclusions follow.

We shall not cover the broad landscape of DeFi, and we shall confine ourselves to the monetary problems raised by new digital coins. We have no ambition to exhaust the economics of blockchain, a task that, after all, may be still out of reach even in principle.

It has been stated that monetary history is an invaluable source of lessons and insights. We do align wholeheartedly with such a remark. Despite the limited size of this work, this attitude is displayed explicitly, most notably in Chapters 2 and 5.

We kindly acknowledge the beautiful support by Tula Weis, Lynnie Sharon, Thangarasan Boopalan, and all the staff at Palgrave. The size and structure of the monograph ("Pivot") has been selected so as to enhance readability and effectiveness in addressing phenomena that have a recent origin and are in rapid evolution.

Parma, Italy
April 2023

Augusto Schianchi
Andrea Mantovi

Contents

Abbreviations

BIS	Bank for International Settlements
BoE	Bank of England
CBDC	Central Bank Digital Currency
DeFi	Decentralized Finance
ECB	European Central Bank
FLP	Fisher-Lynch-Paterson (impossibility theorem)
GST	Global Stabilization Time
IMF	International Monetary Fund
IOU	I Owe You
MM	Modigliani Miller Irrelevance Framework
MMMF	Money Market Mutual Fund
NQA	No Questions Asked (principle of)
PBC	People's Bank of China
PoS	Proof-of-Stake
PoW	Proof-of-Work
SMR	State Machine Replication
SR	Sveriges Riksbank
TSS	Time-Stamping Service

List of Figures

CHAPTER 1

Introduction

Abstract This chapter introduces the methodology that shapes our discussion. We start with the short history of Bitcoin and its followers as digital information transfer mechanisms. The monetary status of such coins is given a preliminary discussion in terms of social credit balances and the ideal pure credit economy. The basic one-shot simultaneous mining game is introduced in its qualitative features. The pattern of cost competitiveness shapes the pattern of strategic entry. Other incentives are briefly discussed, in particular, the incentives to start attacks. Our methodological stance emerges in connection with the specificity of the incentive mechanism generated by the Nakamoto design, that economists are required to stylize in its essence; Leshno and Strack provide a paradigmatic example of such an approach. The monetary problem of the 2020s is given a preliminary glimpse, with due emphasis on the role of central banks in coordinating financial markets and managing the supply of liquidity therein, in connection with the "phase transition" generated by the unconventional monetary policies of the 2010s.

Keyword Bitcoin · Cryptocurrency · Mining · Liquidity · Central bank · Balance sheet

A. Schianchi and A. Mantovi, *The Economics of Cryptocurrencies and Digital Money*, Palgrave Studies in Financial Services Technology,
https://doi.org/10.1007/978-3-031-44248-3_1

A mandatory step of a scientific endeavor is the declaration of the methodology employed. In this chapter, we introduce and motivate our methodological stance, at the same time providing preliminary insights that may help readers move immediately to subsequent chapters in search of particular themes (after all, many readers shall be already acquainted with the working of blockchains, hashing, etc.). We shall be dealing with phenomena that have a recent origin and yet display astonishing richness; with that said, our discussion is essentially theoretical, and meant to build a logic for looking at events. We shall address empirical entities and processes to the extent that they represent structural elements of the phenomenology we are interested in. Needless to say, Bitcoin[1] is the star of the show.

1.1 A Recent History

In the fall of 2008, amid the great financial turmoil, an unknown entity under the pseudonym Satoshi Nakamoto released a white paper describing the Bitcoin "peer-to-peer electronic cash system" as an online architecture powering transactions and record-keeping in a public ledger that develops without a central authority. The decentralized activity of *miners* supports the emergence of decentralized consensus on the history of transactions and ownership distribution of the electronic cash (coins) generated within the architecture itself. The platform is *permissionless*, and the entry of miners is driven by the incentives generated by fixed rewards and variable transaction fees. The platform is *public*, in that participants can scrutinize the flows of information therein.

In January 2009 the Bitcoin platform started operations, with little impact beyond the circle of stakeholders. Subsequently, the phenomenon has progressively raised the interest of a larger audience, beginning perhaps with the computer scientists acknowledging the theoretical innovation of the Nakamoto design, that has been christened *blockchain* (the term does not feature in the paper by Nakamoto). However, the philosophy of freedom from a central authority has been an attitude of a large community of developers of distributed systems for decades. "We reject:

[1] In line with a large part of the literature, we shall refer to both the blockchain and the coin by the same term *Bitcoin*—a number of Authors adopt the lowercase initial letter to denote the coin. Standard notation for the unit of account is BTC, and mBTC (10^{-3}), μBTC (10^{-6}), and *satoshi* (10^{-8}) for subunits.

kings, presidents and voting. We believe in: rough consensus and running code." Already in the late 1980s this commandment (attributed to Dave Clark[2]) featured on t-shirts of participants in the Internet Engineering Task Force.

The Bitcoin architecture coordinates the actions of users and miners along the lines dictated by the protocol. Users create *wallets* that combine a Bitcoin address (a *public key*) and a password (a *private key*). These wallets enable users to manage their endowment of coins and engage in transactions with one another, with 10^{-8} BTC as the smallest subunit of account. Users broadcast the relevant data about transactions, including the value of the fee associated with each transaction. Miners fill *blocks* with such data, starting with the *coinbase transaction* that fixes the reward for the validation of the block. A block with capacity 1 MB can accommodate roughly 2,200 transactions. Block capacity used to range between 1 and 2 MB before the SegWit upgrade increased the size limit to 4 MB in 2017; the Taproot upgrade in 2021 improved on SegWit by batching multiple transactions together and increasing block capacity—the debate on block capacity is a relevant theme in the short history of the Bitcoin community, with challenging strategic implications (see Sect. 4.5). The protocol grants autonomy about which pending transactions to include in a block, and, evidently, miners are attracted by larger transaction fees; fees thereby become bids for block space.

Miners compete for solving the cryptopuzzles associated with blocks, and the share of computational resources deployed by a miner gauges the probability of succeeding according to the Bitcoin *selection rule*. The winner of one such contest is rewarded with the sum of the fixed block reward, consisting of newly minted coins, and the variable sum of the aforementioned transaction fees. The initial fixed block reward of 50 coins has been periodically halved (every 210,000 blocks), so as to follow the geometric progression 50, 25, 12.5, and so on (since May 2020 the fixed block reward is 6.25 coins). The sum of the corresponding geometric series is 100, so that $100 \times 210{,}000 = 21$ million coin is the least upper bound for Bitcoin supply (at the last date of halving, May 2020, the number of coins already minted was 18.375 million). The Bitcoin community is told that by 2140 the minting process should terminate and that the reward of miners shall be confined to transaction fees from

[2] David Dana Clark has been chief protocol architect of the development of the Internet, and has been awarded a number of important prizes for his achievements.

then on. In such respects, it matters to notice that the size of transaction fees has been orders of magnitude smaller than the fixed block reward all along the history of Bitcoin, and that the variable part of the reward of miners has represented a small percentage of the fixed block reward.

The type of cryptopuzzles facing miners, defined by the function SHA-256 (see next chapter), is conceived so as to require brute force computations that represent the sense of Proof-of-Work (PoW) in the Bitcoin arena. Miners force a hash inequality by repeatedly changing the input to the function until output is small enough—specialized hardware has been developed for this task. Once accomplished, the solution, the *hash*, is written on the corresponding block; the community confirms the correctness of the hash and the validation of the block, and all miners update their copies of the ledger. A decentralized consensus is reached about the proper upgrade of the history of transactions recorded in blocks, that are *supposed to be* added in an append-only practice that results in a well-ordered chain of blocks. The record is "immutable" to the extent that altering the history of transactions requires disproportionate costs.

It takes time for the above information transfers to be properly acknowledged by the nodes of the network (this is a fundamental theme of computer science). Different miners may happen to solve a puzzle independently, each of them honestly claiming the reward. There exist procedures to solve these conflicts. "Dishonest" behavior as well is allowed by these delays. More generally, the platform admits phenomena that counter the prescriptions and the objectives of the protocol and can materialize for instance in double-spending or forks. Once a fork has occurred, the *Longest Chain Rule* instructs miners to update the longer chain as the proper continuation of the history of transactions.

This brief description of the Bitcoin design already enables one to access the game theoretic literature and grasp the strategic problems that are generated in a PoW ecology. However, our ambition is also to shed light on the different ways of "trust" that a blockchain and a monetary institution are meant to address. In this respect, in Chapter 2 we shall describe the basic elements of the Nakamoto design.

The ideas developed by Nakamoto (2008) do not come out of the blue. At the turn of the millennium, the economics of information security started to develop systematic maps of the incentives at play along the value chains of information security. The crucial problem is the potential misalignment of incentives between, on the one hand, those in charge of designing or managing the security of a network, and, on the other hand, the ones that suffer (*internalize*, in the jargon of economists) the costs of security failures. One can consider for instance the incentives to develop secure software and the fact that developers are not always paid adequately for developing high-level products. Anderson and Moore (2006) provide an effective review of the basic insights of the discipline, for which the design of peer-to-peer systems is a major target; the Nakamoto design represents a prominent case study. "The tools and concepts of game theory and microeconomics are becoming just as important as the mathematics of cryptography to the security engineer" (ivi).

In our view, the nascent economics of new digital money builds in a twofold perspective. On the one hand, economists are meant to address the incentives and network effects at play in a blockchain ecology. In particular, the incentives for miners to enter the ecology and behave honestly are the major innovation of the Nakamoto design. Among other things, both academics and columnists have pointed out the strategic relevance of the variable costs of performing computational tasks: these costs will play a decisive role in our game theoretic discussion—on empirical grounds, the effects on the profitability of mining of the exit of Chinese miners in 2021 have been well documented in specialized media.

On the other hand, the problematic monetary status of new digital tokens is what researchers and policymakers are targeting in their respective efforts to uncover the theoretical and empirical subtleties involved in the proliferation of these instruments both as means of payment and stores of value. Notice that the terms "coin" and "token" have been recently differentiated with respect to the functions performed on a blockchain; still, as economists, we follow the tradition in which a *token* is a form of money that differentiates from *account-based* money; in this sense, an ancient gold coin and a modern banknote are tokens in the same sense (see for instance Carstens, 2019). Well, it is from the monetary perspective that one appreciates the relevance of the price dynamics of cryptocurrencies.

Strong incentives must have been at play in the early emergence of the necessity of converting Bitcoins in other payment instruments—among other things, the variable costs of mining activity had to be paid, with all probability, in standard currencies. An ecology soon developed of entities performing such exchanges (early players being Mr. Gox, BTC-e, Bitstamp, and Bitfinex). "Prices" of Bitcoin thereby emerged as exchange rates with currencies (one writes BTCUSD for the exchange rate with the US dollar).

It is largely appreciated that the price dynamics of Bitcoin is a key factor of the crypto eruption, and it is worth having some dates at hand.

2013 between October and November a sudden increase from around $150 to more than $1000 takes place, followed by a dramatic fall.

2017 A rally takes price again above $1,000 in March. At the turn of the year $18,000 is in sight.

2021 in April the all-time high of about $65,000 is reached, followed by ample fluctuations and again well above $60,000 in November.

2022 the downfall, from a peak of roughly $46,000 in April to less than $17,000 at the turn of the year.

2023 price increases above $24,000 in February, then falls below $21,000 but then increases again and reaches above $30,000 in July.

The volatility of the Bitcoin price, that displayed clearly in the charts available online, has been acknowledged as a property of cryptocurrencies in general. A number of Authors have been trying to separate speculative and purchasing effects in order to investigate the drivers of this price dynamics, a task that is far from straightforward and calls for a number of assumptions that may be questioned. In search of a theoretical setting for addressing the phenomenon, it has been recently postulated that the price of Bitcoin does reflect some economic "fundamentals," namely, the stream of net transactional benefits (Biais et al., 2023). A disconnect with macro variables has been observed (see Benigno and Rosa, 2023). We shall not enter this newly conceived approaches, and rather focus on the consequences of this price volatility, concerning both the potential of cryptocurrencies of rivaling standard payment systems, and the monetary status of "stablecoins" as tokens meant to be unaffected by such volatility problems.

Beyond the price dynamics, a number of interesting phenomena characterize the history of Bitcoin, which unfolds with the exogenous scheme fixed in the protocol, key features being permissionless entry, the PoW mechanism, and the fact that the blockchain is programmed to grow at a steady pace, irrespective of the number of computational resources at play. This goal is achieved by a periodical (every 2016 hashes) adjustment of the difficulty of puzzles, so as to maintain a rate of block validation of roughly one every 10 minutes, or 144 per day, so that adjustment occurs roughly every two weeks (evidently, scalability is not among the objectives of this design).

To appreciate that such an adjustment is necessary, one can look at plots of the exponential increase of the Bitcoin *hashrate*, namely, the number of tentative hashes per second (this unit is written H/s) generated by miners at play. The hashrate is a good measure of the overall computational power at play at a definite instant, provided one assumes that different miners operate hardware that is homogeneous in hashing performance (specific hardware has been developed for this brute force task).

In parallel with these exogenous features, though, noticeable endogenous emergent phenomena have characterized the history of Bitcoin, like the many forks that have occured (more than one hundred by 2023), the strategic partial filling of blocks, or the concentration of mining activity in pools (recent charts of the Bitcoin hashrate feature as major players Foundry USA, AntPool, F2Pool, Binance Pool and ViaBTC). The emerging economics of cryptocurrencies is largely devoted to the discussion of these endogenous effects pertaining to the Bitcoin ecology as paradigmatic.[3] Well, we shall find it useful to deepen the endogenous nature of the global (aggregate) hashrate by making it the *pivotal* degree of freedom of the strategic problems within a PoW blockchain—this is not to say that the hashrate is to be considered a "cause," or a "determinant," of phenomena. In these respects, it matters that there exist open access exact figures of the aggregate hashrate, and common knowledge about the properness of such figures.

The history of crypto unfolds with the introduction of a large number of *altcoins*, part of which explicitly meant to surpass Bitcoin in some dimension—some of which originated by hard forks of the Bitcoin blockchain. For instance, Monero is meant to surpass Bitcoin in the secrecy/anonymity dimension. The explosive demand for these new tokens, together with the proliferation of dedicated intermediaries, has been considered motivation enough for acknowledging a new class of "cryptoassets," deserving monitoring and economic inquiry. In parallel,

[3] Along similar lines, researchers are often interested in the properties of US financial markets as the more developed and therefore more significant. With that said, the comparability of markets poses serious methodological challenges.

a rapid evolution of blockchain applications has taken place, progressively uncovering the potential of the Nakamoto breakthrough.

In 2013 a white paper by Vitalik Buterin (this time, not a pseudonymous entity) introduced the Ethereum project, that raised over $18 million in Bitcoin in 2014. The platform started operations in 2015. Ethereum has been considered a sort of counterpart of Bitcoin, in that its ambition amply surpasses the objectives of the Bitcoin blockchain. The Ethereum Virtual Machine is a Turing-complete execution environment that supports the cryptocurrency Ether but also higher level operations like smart contracts (see Davidson, 2023). Connected with this technology is the short history of the Decentralized Autonomous Organization. The Ethereum hashing algorithm has been conceived as not to admit specialized hardware to boost performance in the PoW challenge. In 2022, Ethereum has switched from PoW to *Proof-of-Stake* (PoS).

A follower of Ethereum is Cardano,[4] among whose developers one acknowledges Charles Hoskinson, co-founder of Ethereum. The Cardano blockchain employs PoS and features the native token ADA, which is often referred to as Cardano itself. The platform claims a visionary mission of pursuing positive global change and "redistribute power from unaccountable structures to individuals." One further notices the advent of the Stellar Development Foundation with the Lumen token, which has been primarily conceived as an intermediation device, rather than a means of payment.

Overall, the development of the crypto ecology manifests itself in several dimensions. An increasing number of official businesses, both retail and wholesale, now accept transactions in Bitcoin and other tokens. Credit cards are now available for withdrawing cash or buying crypto on major platforms. Bitcoin has been adopted as the official currency by El Salvador in 2021 and the Central African Republic in 2022. Arguably, a unique mix of profit opportunities, market glamor, technological innovation, conceptual challenges, and aspirations to justice is the chemical reaction that fueled the crypto euphoria of the last decade. The new discipline of "Tokenomics" is blossoming at the crossroads of economics and computer science. The recent crypto downfall has decisively calmed the euphoria. With that said, it is of great interest that Bitcoin implements an

[4] Gerolamo Cardano was an Italian mathematician of the sixteenth century renowned for polyhedric interests and activities.

innovative mechanism for achieving "decentralized consensus" about the settlement of exchanges that take place therein.

As pointed out by Davidson (2023), before the introduction of Bitcoin it was believed that decentralized consensus in a distributed system should require a *permissioned* setting in which nodes were fixed and recognizable. Bitcoin has been the first distributed system supporting the emergence of consensus among a variable number of nodes that can enter and exit the network with no permission; to date, its real-world test is unrivaled.

The Bitcoin platform differentiates substantially from standard payment systems, and also from the foundational features of distributed systems. Still, that blockchains represent a genuine revolution has been questioned. It has been conjectured that off-chain control may have played, and still play, a pivotal role in the governance of activities, effectively regimenting the (allegedly) self-regulating dynamics of decentralized consensus and protocol adjustment even in a permissionless blockchain. The definition itself of the blockchain may not be taken as settled. One should not underestimate issues of definition, since different incentives and objectives may be at stake. Some definitions of blockchain encompass desired outcomes, like the immutability of the record, and this is somewhat turning things upside down.

The desirability of a new decentralized payment system is declared by Nakamoto (2008) himself in terms of some weaknesses of the trust based model, but a more philosophical position advocates the desirability of decentralized consensus with respect to the submission to the power of established financial institutions like banks. The absence of a single point of failure has also been pointed out among the merits of the new design. Well, the form of "privacy" or "anonymity" shared by participants to the Bitcoin network seems to be pivotal for the convenience yield of the system, in which authentication of legal identity is not required.

This point raises subtle issues on information-theoretic grounds, on which one distinguishes issues of anonymity, pseudonymity, and linkability. "Bitcoin is designed to allow its users to send and receive payments with an acceptable level of privacy as well as any other form of money. However, Bitcoin is not anonymous and cannot offer the same level of privacy as cash" (Bitcoin.org). Bitcoin is said to be pseudonymous, the pseudonym being the address for receiving coins. But if the pseudonym is linked to one's identity... We refer to Narayanan et al. (2016) for an engaging discussion of these problems.

Ideally, it would be nice to draw a clear-cut separation between the information-theoretic computer science and the economics of blockchain. We are not in a position to draw one such line and shall adopt lines of reasoning that seem to approach the problem of trust with apparent soundness. It is a fact that economists are forced to employ brutal simplifications that may let down computer scientists. As an example, Leshno and Strack (2020) reduce the anonymity of miners to the symmetry of the selection rule. It is a major theme of our monograph to motivate such simplifications, which may be considered among the reasons why economics is referred to as the dismal science.

The potential of blockchain applications and DeFi seems enormous, if only for the billion-dollar investments that have been set in place in recent years. Still, in what follows, we shall concentrate on the game theory of PoW as the natural starting point of a theoretical inquiry on cryptocurrencies. Within a few years, PoS may rise to a comparable status. We shall explore the very essence of the blockchain construct in Chapter 2, disregarding important building blocks like Merkle trees and significant themes like the mechanics of hard and soft forks, that do not fit in our sharp economic perspective (needless to say, this is not to underestimate the relevance of these points). The problem of the monetary status of new digital tokens, however, is worth immediate introduction. The problem of money is in its essence a problem of trust, and, as the saying goes, trust can't be taken on trust.

1.1.1 Digital Information Transfer and Pure Credit

According to Andolfatto and Martin (2022), in order to "decode" the nature of new digital tokens, one can interpret cryptocurrencies as digital information transfer mechanisms. The information-theoretic computer science of blockchain does support this interpretation; still, on monetary grounds, information-theoretic aspects do matter to the extent that they relate to problems of trust. Decentralization of consensus building poses subtle challenges to the monetary interpretation of the tokens within a blockchain, and, no wonder, scholars look for analogies with more established settings.

To begin with, Andolfatto and Martin (2022) notice that there exist simple enough situations in which trust is sustained by continued social interactions. "In small communities, individual consumption and production decisions can be debited and credited, respectively, in a sort of communal ledger of action histories. This is because it is relatively easy for everyone to monitor and record individual actions. A person who has produced mightily for the group builds social credit. Large social credit balances can be "spent" later as consumption (favors drawn from other members of the community)" (ivi). An analogy with cryptocurrencies develops along the following lines.

A cryptocurrency is a means of exchange within its own blockchain. The token has no recognizable economic fundamentals underlying (despite visions on expected streams of benefits), and yet is accepted as payment instrument and accounted for in the wallets of individual users. In turn, users are self-selected, whether permissionless or permissioned the blockchain may be; after all, no one is forced to enter a blockchain (on the contrary, most users of standard currencies are not self-selected, and have no choice of the currency with which to pay taxes). Therefore, for a number of reasons, most entrants (user and miners) may have *ex ante* substantial trust in the correctness of counterparties and well functioning of the system.

One can stylize this setting as a *pure credit* economy, i.e. one in which trust, for some reason, can be taken for granted, and there exists a shared log of reciprocal debits and credits upon which decentralized consensus is continuously renewed. An intuitive example is provided by a rural economy of barter in which neighbors have perfect trust of one another and exchange their products at definite relative prices.[5] In this economy, *I owe you* (IOU) notes, as record-keeping of transactions, may even circulate in order to solve the problem of the double coincidence of maturity of products—milk 'matures' every day, whereas peaches mature with a longer delay—a coincidence that resembles the more traditional problem of double coincidence of wants. Analogously, a crypto token can be taken to represent an IOU that circulates as a device of shared accounting and information transfer.

Evidently, this picture is too stylized to represent a satisfactory description of the monetary status of a coin within its own blockchain, but this is exactly the point. Recall, the frictionless ideal setting depicted by Modogliani and Miller in the 1950s is a stage upon which to represent different plots. Somehow analogously, the ideal picture of the pure credit

[5] Perhaps in a general equilibrium framework represented by Edgeworth boxes.

economy disregards monetary problems of trust, and rather concentrates on the technology of information transfer. In fact, we shall find in Chapter 2 that computer scientists and monetary economists are meant to address *different* problems of "trust" that the extant literature may not have disentangled with due emphasis. This differentiation is the major inspiration of our work.

1.1.2 The Crypto Downfall

"Contrary to the decentralization narrative, crypto often relies on unregulated intermediaries that pose financial risks" (BIS, 2022). These risks have materialized, and in November 2022 the crypto market has collapsed. In previous months serious episodes had already shaken the foundations of the industry, most notably the Terra/Luna fall in May. Then, in November, the crack of the cryptoexchange FTX, that was valued $32 billions, marks the spectacular crash of the system. The media have covered the drama of investors waking up with their funds locked into collapsed crypto lenders, and a number of columnists have gone all out in commenting on the fall from grace of Sam Bankman-Fried (the founder and boss of FTX) and denouncing the consequences of the "cryptofrenzy."

At the time of writing (Spring 2023) these events do not seem to have undermined the foundations of established environments like Bitcoin or Ethereum. Still, in the words of the Economist (2023, November 19–25), the mess has let down supporters, embarrassed investors, and made fools of politicians. The future of cryptocurrencies is uncertain. For our purposes, it matters to point out that the downfall is to a large extent a crisis of crypto as collateral.

In a preliminary assessment of events, The Economist reports evidences of poor accounting practices and poor quality of the assets held by FTX (among which positions in "shitcoins"). Relevant to the story is the link with Alameda, a major counterparty of FXT, also owned by Mr. Bankman-Fried. There exist narratives about Alameda using poor coins as collateral for raising funds from FTX, in order to move to positions in more reliable tokens like Bitcoin or stablecoins. Mr. Bankman-Fried himself, in an interview with Bloomberg, described how to build tokens and use them as collateral for raising funds. Plain good sense envisions problems with these practices; however, it is our aim to provide systematic conceptual backing for appreciating the generality of the problem of proper collateralization, in connection with the fundamental monetary principle of "no questions asked" (NQA).

Practices of using tokens as collateral, evidently, have nothing to do with the ambitions of DeFi of financial inclusion. In fact, these practices do not pertain to the physiology of PoW (that we introduce in the following section) and have no role in the philosophy of decentralized consensus of escaping standard monetary arrangements.

1.2 A Game Theoretic Approach

Economic sciences are profoundly shaped by issues of decentralization, witness the metaphor of the invisible hand coined by Adam Smith in the celebrated treatise on the wealth of nations of 1776. The theory of general economic equilibrium elaborated by Kenneth Arrow and Gerard Debreu in the 1950s is considered a consistent game theoretic representation of the inherently decentralized perfectly competitive market mechanism, under the ideal assumptions of price taking, perfect information and frictionless adjustment of production and consumption choices. The way this decentralization works in practice has been a continuous intellectual challenge for economists, which has shaped a large part of the history of economic thought. One can recall for instance the tale of the mythological auctioneer conceived by Leon Walras, and the analytical representation of exchange in the "box" developed by Vilfredo Pareto and Francis Ysidro Edgeworth. Given this background in economic decentralization, economists should find it stimulating to look for an "invisible hand" in the background of the design conceived by Nakamoto.

In the words of Narayanan et al. (2016), decentralization is not all or nothing. No system is purely centralized or decentralized, and various aspects of the Bitcoin mechanism fall on different points of the centralization-decentralization spectrum. Analogous statements can be predicated on economic systems. Think of the different properties of different markets, in which buyers and sellers manage to agree on prices and terms of transactions by means of mechanisms that display various features along the centralization-decentralization spectrum. For instance, readers may find it stimulating to recall the properties of stock markets and their place in the spectrum; think of the selection of the stocks that can be traded (the conditions for initial public offering), the operation of dealers that manage order flows and quote bid-ask spreads, and the operation of analysts releasing reports and forecasts. With these insights in the background, economists may find it engaging to elaborate on the centralization-decentralization spectrum of Nakamoto consensus.

A burgeoning literature adopts game theory as the language for discussing PoW. Recall, game theory is a mathematical framework for representing strategic interactions with parsimony. One can fix the number of players and the order of moves, possibly simultaneous. Nodes and information sets depict the map of the ways the interaction may unfold; beliefs gauge the weights that players attach to different states of the world; finally, definite payoffs gauge the preferences of players over outcomes (it is typical to consider payoffs as numbers, but a class of games ranks outcomes in terms of *win* or *lose*). These are the basic exogenous elements of a model game that researchers can employ to stylize the economic setting under inspection. One is then in a position to uncover the endogenous properties of the model, starting with the pattern of best responses and the set of Nash equilibria. We assume the reader familiar enough with basic notions like normal and extensive forms, best responses, Nash equilibria, and backward induction, and refer to Binmore (2007) for an excellent discussion.

Recall, at a Nash equilibrium players adopt reciprocal best responses, so that no player can gain from unilateral deviation from the current strategy. This general notion has been refined in many ways, and we will find it proper to digress on backward induction in Chapter 4, if only for the role played by this concept in the burgeoning game theoretic literature on PoW, that addresses the competition among miners at varying levels of sophistication. A whole taxonomy of games and Nash equilibria representing relevant phenomena (like the strategic interaction of users and miners, the concentration in mining, investment in specialized hardware, forks, etc.) is being compiled. Such a "horizontal" perspective for sure has merits; still, our approach is "vertical," in the sense of aiming at a hierarchical picture of increasing complexity.

Theoretical research typically involves the *reduction* of the properties of a system to a (hopefully small) number of fundamental degrees of freedom, in terms of whose interactions one hopes to *construct* the observable properties of the system. The goal may be truly hard; *more is different* in the celebrated expression coined by Philip Warren Anderson (think of constructing molecular biology out of chemistry). However, we shall reduce the game theory of PoW to a foundational rent-seeking competition, and then, building on the extant literature, envision elaborations of the basic game form that enable the representation of emergent phenomena, and, possibly, the elaboration of right questions on superior levels of complexity, like the scalability of a PoW environment. Despite the aspiration for democracy and decentralization embodied by the Nakamoto philosophy, the Bitcoin ecology has turned into an oligopoly of a few mining pools, whose coalition may enable them to freeze funds and alter the record at will. Game theory enables one to represent such an occurrence as an equilibrium outcome of the competition in place at varying levels of complexity, starting with the basic game of PoW (Arnosti and Weinberg, 2019); more articulated models target different layers of complexity of this emergent phenomenon. Let us introduce the foundational relevance of the basic mining game.

The game is one-shot, namely, it does not repeat itself as the real competition of miners does—it goes without saying that the analysis of a repeated game builds on the properties of the stage game, which must therefore be studied exhaustively in isolation. In a baseline interpretation, the stage game is repeated indefinitely, and its Nash equilibrium represents a steady state equilibrium activity for heterogenous miners. The game is simultaneous, i.e. players do not observe the choices of opponents before making their moves; still, the notion of *best response* is well-defined in simultaneous settings and will represent a focus of our discussion. Players (miners) compete over *quantities*, namely, the computational resources deployed, that in a PoW environment can be measured by hashrates. The analogy with Cournot oligopolies is already largely established.

The game is stochastic, in the sense that the outcome is not deterministically determined by the actions of players, and rather emerges as an instance of a probability distribution fixed by the selection rule, according to which the share of resources deployed by a player fixes the probability with which the same player turns out to win the competition (a *contest*). Players are assumed to be risk-neutral in order to fix the *expected utility* benchmark level of analysis. Payoffs coincide with expected rewards minus costs. Players are identical in the selection rule (this is crucial to the democracy of decentralized consensus) and it is costs that differentiate miners in their competitiveness. With simple enough cost functions, one obtains a well-defined ranking of the competitiveness of players.

The game admits a unique Nash equilibrium in pure strategies, and it is not difficult to anticipate that more efficient miners should display larger activity levels in equilibrium. The problem of entry is not explicitly represented in this simultaneous game and is rather implicitly encoded in the choice of activity level, so as to let the term "entry" denote switching from vanishing to positive activity level at a definite aggregate hashrate, and the other way round for the term "exit."

An intuitive insight into the foundational nature of the basic game concerns its *cardinal* payoffs, which represent precise quantitative measures of the expected profit prospect facing miners, and as such witness the sharp definition of the elementary interaction under inquiry. More elaborate games have more qualitative significance and employ 'quasi-cardinal' or even *ordinal* payoffs, with more nuanced interpretations.

A more sophisticated and *crucial* insight concerns the *additive aggregation* property, namely, the fact that players, despite being in general heterogeneous, can be considered to respond to the overall (aggregate) scale of mining activity, in close analogy with Cournot oligopolies, despite their deterministic nature. The aggregate scale of activity is a pivot of our discussion. The additive aggregation property follows from the symmetry of the PoW selection rule and is crucial to the analytical tractability of the problem. Noticeably, ongoing research progresses are shedding increasing light on the implications of aggregation for the endogenous properties of such games, as well as for deepening the political economy of contests.

The above properties enable Leshno and Strack (2020) to pin down the theoretical relevance of the basic game in terms of three independent foundational properties of PoW, namely, a stylized notion of anonymity, the absence of incentives for risk-neutral miners to consolidate, and the absence of incentives to assume multiple fake identities. The Authors establish that any protocol meant to share these features should adopt the Bitcoin selection rule.

With these considerations, we are undertaking the economic mission of stylization. With the exception of stochasticity, neither of the above properties seems to represent a sound description of the real competition among miners, and yet one should not find it paradoxical that the resulting picture turns out to represent a good lens for looking at phenomena. In May 2021 China outlawed the intensively energy-consuming activity of Bitcoin mining, and a substantial fraction of miners has abandoned the scene. Specialized media (see for instance Szalay, 2021) have adequately covered the positive impact of such a "crackdown" on the profitability of mining, stimulating the entry of new (possibly, less competitive) players from different parts of the globe. The following subsection introduces our theoretical vision of this empirical process.

1.2.1 Competitiveness, Exit, and Best Responses

It is an elementary guess that when a number of players exit a market, competition weakens and barriers to entry soften. It is more elaborate to envision exit sequences as the best responses of an explicit model game. Well, recent results by Mantovi (2021) enable us to plot competitive advantages and exit thresholds in terms of the aggregate best responses of the basic mining game, for which we anticipate some intuitions (full treatment in Chapter 3) so as to make our conceptual journey more transparent.

Consider 4 miners endowed with linear homogeneous cost functions, thereby uniquely identified by the marginal cost parameter. These parameters induce a well-defined ranking of the competitiveness of players. Each player can be further characterized by an index of competitiveness, ranging between 0 and 1, as a function of the aggregate level of activity (this is an original element of our approach). The value 1 characterizes maximal competitiveness and is attained in the limit of vanishing activity; the value 0 triggers the evaporation of competitiveness, and therefore exit. The sum of individual indices is an aggregate index X of the competitiveness of the four miners, and ranges, evidently, between 0 and 4.

Figure 1.1 depicts a story in which the index X (the variable on the vertical axis) starts with maximal value 4 in the limit of vanishing aggregate activity s (the variable on the horizontal axis). With increasing s, the competitiveness of all players lower, but players with inferior competitiveness face a steeper descent. The least competitive player is the first to hit an exit threshold, which corresponds to the first change in the slope of the line. Three players remain, with the (now) least competitive one being the first to hit the next exit threshold. The story unfolds analogously for the remaining players until activity ceases at all once the last (the more competitive) players exit. Notice the intuitive feature that there must exist an upper bound to the level of activity at which miners find it economic to operate since the reward is fixed, whereas costs increase linearly with the level of activity.

To sum up, with the increase in the aggregate activity level s, miners sequentially (from the least to the more competitive) exit the industry.

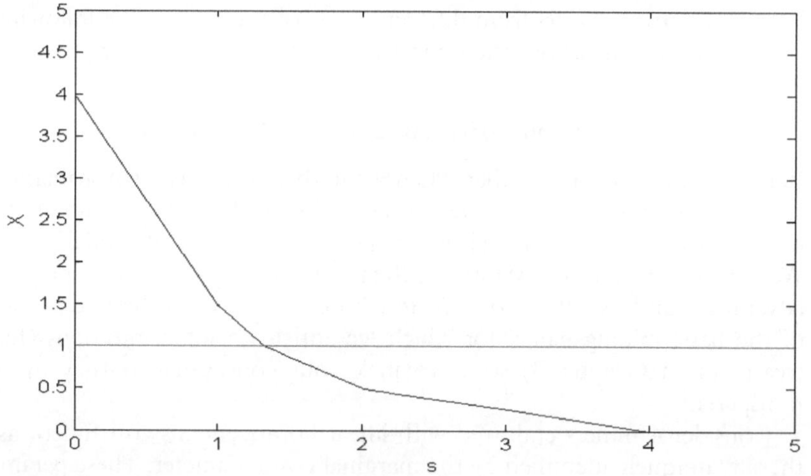

Fig. 1.1 Plot of the decrease of individual activity and competitive advantages with the increase of the aggregate scale of activity

The transparent graphical representation (that the extant literature does not seem to feature) pins down sharp strategic insights on the empirical evidence about new miners entering the Bitcoin industry in spring 2021.

In a figure corresponding to the one above, the exit of Chinese miners corresponds to a shift to the left of the current value of the variable s, but also to a new piecewise linear pattern for the index X. By far, these considerations have been developed qualitatively, but in Chapter 3 shall be given exhaustive analytical treatment. However, already at this intuitive level, one can build preliminary intuitions about the way a ban on the more efficient miners results in a curve with traits of steeper descent, and an equilibrium featuring, in general, less efficient miners.

The extant game theoretic literature on PoW focuses on the characterization of Nash equilibria. In fact, Arnosti and Weinberg (2019) employ the index X (albeit with a different argument) in order to establish that the Nash equilibrium of the game is attained for $X = 1$ (corresponding to the horizontal red line in the plot); in our example, only the two more efficient miners are at play (deploy resources) in the unique Nash equilibrium of the system, and the more efficient one displays larger activity level. At this Nash equilibrium all four players best respond to the strategies of opponents, so that no player would gain from a unilateral deviation from his strategy.

These properties of the equilibrium of the contest are well known, but Mantovi (2021) establishes an exact analytic link between the index X and the index Υ defined by Szidarovszky and Okuguchi (1997) as the difference between aggregate best responses and current activity (so that the condition for Nash equilibrium can be written $\Upsilon = 0$). One is then in a position to uncover the connection between the different characterizations of the Nash equilibrium of the system, in terms of X or Υ, and thereby shed further light on the significance of the condition $X = 1$. The very possibility of drawing plots like the one above is founded on these results, in which the function X compares with Υ (i.e. has the same argument) in fixing the best responses of the system, and therefore its Nash equilibria.

These preliminary insights project us to the core of our methodological approach. The strategic problem of PoW is a competition in which strategic advantages originate primarily from cost competitiveness and manifest themselves in different exit (entry) thresholds. This is a more insightful view than a sharp characterization of the unique Nash equilibrium of the system. Truly sophisticated questions pertain to the extent to which a definite state of the world can be depicted as a Nash equilibrium of some model game. To develop a map of the best responses of the game is only part of the story, but certainly a relevant part. Consider the following analogy.

It is well known that perfect knowledge of the rules of chess does not make you a grandmaster. The complexity of the game makes the strategic space unchartable. Over the centuries, a massive body of theory has been elaborated concerning best openings, principles of medium play (like positional play, the logic of sacrifices, etc.), and finals, with some simple enough final admitting a description of perfect play. Players employ and interpret these pieces of the global chart,[6] and progressively develop a sensibility concerning the missing parts of the map.

Somehow analogously, the complexity of the implications of PoW can only be partially enlightened by the Nash equilibria of specific games. It takes a more general exploration of the strategic space to develop

[6] Interestingly, artificial players like Stockfish are mapping new areas of this strategic space.

educated insights concerning out-of-equilibrium responses. Our monograph targets this conceptual level not only for the strategic problems raised by a blockchain protocol. For instance, the introduction of central bank digital currency is a game that does not reduce to the elaboration of guidelines concerning the efficiency of a desired equilibrium conceived as *already attained*. An upgraded monetary system is different, and may display unanticipated tensions and undesirable adjustments. This is a game that policymakers want to *coordinate* toward an equilibrium of smooth functioning. The recent policies of "forward guidance" by major central banks manifest explicitly the relevance of coordination in the evolution of market dynamics. Well, advocates of decentralized consensus seem to pursue the idea that technology may enable one to short-circuit the inherently centralized instances of coordination and stabilization of markets. "Indeed, private sector innovation benefits society precisely because it is built on the strong foundations of the central bank" (BIS, 2020). Furthermore, decentralized consensus generates incentives that can undermine its own existence.

1.2.2 *Other Incentives*

The above preliminary account of the one-shot mining game displays basic features of the *physiology* of mining competition, that follows the lines dictated by the protocol. Well, researches have already gone a long way in discussing incentives that counter the design and the objectives of the protocol and can materialize as "attacks." Nakamoto (2008) himself states in the first page of the paper that the Bitcoin system is secure as long as honest nodes collectively control more CPU power than any cooperating group of attacker nodes. The security itself of the system, therefore, is a strategic problem.

Halaburda et al. (2022) provide a sharp account of this topic, and we refer the reader to the original article for an authoritative review of the microeconomics of cryptocurrencies. The Authors review the economic literature on forks, in particular, Kroll et al. (2013) and Biais et al. (2019), and then address the incentives that underlie attacks. In the first instance, economists are required to address attacks as stylized incentive problems that have little to do with the technology at play and the specific operations involved. Researchers have therefore primarily concentrated on participation constraints and incentive-compatibility conditions, which represent the pillars of the theory of incentives. Budish (2018) in particular fixes these conditions in quite general terms; noticeably, Budish seems to be the first to emphasize the relevance of distinguishing between "flow attacks" and "stock attacks", that is, attacks that target block rewards (flows) or balances of coins or entire branches of the chain (stocks).

Budish considers the essential parameters that shape the incentives to participate honestly in the ecology, namely, the number N of participants, the block reward θ in terms of native coins, the exchange rate e of the coin with the reference currency (so that expected reward from mining can be written $e\theta\ /N$, under the assumption that players are symmetric in their mining competitiveness) Then, one writes c for the reference cost of operation. One can then write the relevant participation constraint (as a simple cost-expected benefit threshold) as

$$\frac{e\theta}{N} \geq c$$

One then considers the compatibility of this condition with the incentives to behave dishonestly. One introduces some more parameters. A parameter A gauges the fraction of global computational resources required for an attack to work; a parameter V gauges the benefits of the attack; a parameter t denotes the number of blocks that should be validated during the time the attack takes place. One can then write the incentive compatibility condition

$$Nc \geq \frac{V + te\theta}{At}$$

as the condition for an attack not to be profitable. The above pair of conditions can be used to build insights into the robustness of the network. Halaburda et al. (2022) notice that Chiu and Koeppl (2017) establish a no double-spending constraint that compares to these conditions. One can further address the design of efficient parameters.

True, there is much more than incentive theory that economics can contribute to the understanding of blockchain. For instance, Catalini and Gans (2020) address the network effects at play in a blockchain ecology by focusing on a pair of relevant degrees of freedom at play, namely, verification costs and networking costs. A reduction in verification costs is what paves the way for Bitcoin and the like to settle transactions without an intermediary, whereas a reduction in the costs of networking is what allowed these systems to scale in the first place. One can take both costs into consideration and build a story about the way a blockchain ecosystem exploits the benefits of network effects without recourse to a central authority. Within the blockchain, a native token plays a role that compares to that of equity for founders and early employees of a startup. With that said, one admits that permissionless networks still need off-chain governance and coordination between the key stakeholders in order to modify the protocol or respond to an attack.

One then envisions a broader perspective in which game theory provides a consistent language for embedding individual incentives within collective phenomena representing "social norms." Most participants in a blockchain can be argued to see themselves as stakeholders, and a notion of *going concern* for the continuation of the network seems appropriate—the expression *vested interest* has also been employed. The implications of the self-selection of entrants can perhaps be complemented with some notion of "preference for continuation." After all, there is much more to friendship than a continuously renewed cost-benefit analysis. There exist narratives according to which, in the attempt to resolve a fork, some stakeholders gave up on large endowments of coins in order to facilitate the emergence of agreement on one continuation of the chain. Perhaps, dishonest behavior and attacks may be depicted as exit options of some games in which the nuances of the strategic problem may be given a detailed representation.

The industrial economics of the automotive sector does not envision car accidents as a pivotal phenomenon in the evolution of the horizontal and vertical structures of the market. Somehow analogously, pathologies like "attacks" lie outside the major focus of our discussion, in that they do not represent factors that determine the horizontal and vertical structures of the ecology. One can browse Sect. 4.4 on mining pools in order to focus on the kind of industry problems we are interested in. This is not, evidently, to underestimate the relevance of forks and attacks.

Forks have occurred, sure. More than a hundred forks, some of which unintended, have already affected the Bitcoin blockchain. However, these forks represent exceptional events that do not seem to play a significant role in the physiology of the system. Analogously, other forms of attacks may have already materialized, but do not seem to threaten the activity of the more established blockchains (at least, not as the problems underlying the recent crypto downfall). In a sense, an analysis of the pathologies of a blockchain resembles an analysis of the operational risk of banks, that for sure is relevant, but is not what monetary economists and policymakers are primarily interested in. In the design of the future monetary system (see Chapter 5) the aforementioned attacks are not the worries of policymakers; even a cryptocurrency perfectly safe from attacks may not fit the standards of the international monetary arena.

1.3 A Monetary Arena

The Bank of England has publicly stated that a general-purpose digital currency, a digital pound, is likely to be needed within a few years (the expression *Britcoin* is already circulating). Many central banks display a comparable attitude, and some have already taken decisive steps in such a direction. These efforts can be considered the flip side of the coin of the crypto eruption of the last decade. It is our aim to build a monetary perspective on these phenomena.

The current reflection on the future of digital money stages different debates with heterogeneous relevance. Discussions about the desirability of new digital tokens (whether public or privately produced) as substitutes for physical cash are somewhat peripheral to the criticalities raised by new digital instruments; much more cogent is the inquiry about the (alleged) advantages of stablecoins over well established digital payment networks like credit cards or mobile applications, and the elucidation of the principles for regulating such tokens. In order to build a vision on such problems, in this section we introduce the monetary problem of the 2020s, namely, the global problem of *liquidity* that we inherited from the great financial crisis of 2007–2009.

There is a *hierarchy* of monetary institutions that unfolds as a network of balance sheets that channel flows of funds, much like there is a network of arteries and veins through which blood flows in our bodies. This architecture has a delicate physiology and must be upgraded with extreme care in order to avoid systemic clashes. The disordered growth of the shadow banking system at the turn of the millennium is an example of how a monetary system can develop spontaneously in ways that do not represent a sustainable physiology (since 2012 the Financial Stability Board releases a yearly global monitoring report on shadow banking; the expression "shadow banking" has been substituted with "non-bank financial intermediation" in 2018). Payment systems are crucial elements of the network of monetary institutions.

Monetary systems are hierarchical ('vertical') structures with central banks as ultimate sources of liquidity. That liquidity must have an ultimate source, and that there must exist *lenders of last resort*, is by now quite undisputed. This point has been decisively reaffirmed by Ben Bernanke[7] in interviews concerning his mandate at the Fed during the crisis, acknowledging the properness of the analysis of Walter Bagehot (1873), in particular the advice ("Bagethot rule") of lending freely, at a high rate, against good collateral amid a financial panic. The Fed has been adapting this dictum to the modern structure of financial arrangements.

The crisis has reshaped the vision of economists and policymakers on the role of central banks, and the relevance of this new stance is continuously reaffirmed. "The monetary and financial architecture needs solid foundations, just as a skyscraper does. And it is the central bank's role to establish these foundations [...] The monetary system is founded on trust in the currency [...] Central banks amplify efforts of private sector innovators by giving them a solid base to build on" (Carstens, 2019). It is scarcely surprising to acknowledge the fierce opposition of US authorities in recent years to the introduction of Facebook money that would completely circumvent existing circuits. Among other things, the monetary order is part of the geopolitical (dynamic) equilibrium; monetary arrangements have both political influence within countries and strategic implications across borders.

It matters to notice that, amid the turmoil, the Fed has not only been playing the lender but also the *dealer* of last resort in subsequent rounds of quantitative easing programs that have been progressively increasing the size of its balance sheet, according to Fig. 1.2 below. One reads from the plot the huge and progressive increase of bank reserves that have flooded the market with liquidity.

One further notices the additional expansion initiated in 2020 connected with the pandemic. Other central banks have embarked on similar paths. These innovative balance sheet policies (that complement more traditional interest rate policies) were premised on the intent to reverse the path of expansion some day and return to sizes of balance sheets resembling the pre-2007 period. This path reversal has proved unfeasible, and the system has adapted to the new conditions of ample liquidity.

[7] The academic and central banker has been awarded the 2022 Nobel prize in Economic Sciences.

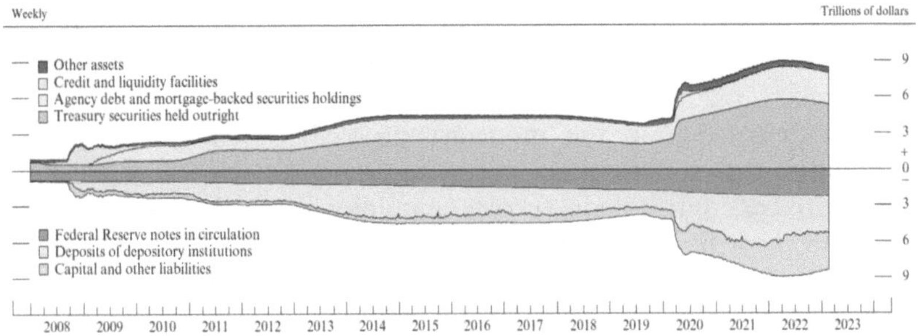

Fig. 1.2 The size and composition of the balance sheet of the Fed since 2008, with assets above and liabilities below. Reproduced from the Monetary Policy Report of March 2023

There exist of course 'horizontal' (we may say ***decentralized***) arrangements that support the stability of positions meant to be safe, in first instance collateralization. In recent years the flows of collateral have been acknowledged as crucial for the functioning of the contemporary financial system, still, the centralized protection given by explicit guarantees (like deposit insurance) is unrivaled in fixing states of "no questions asked" (NQA). Financial stability is a game against panic for which the model of bank runs developed by Diamond and Dybvig (1983) provides a landmark representation. The model displays the reasons why, in order to attain a state of NQA, there must be mechanisms in place. Such a well-established analysis provides a cogent point of view on the recent turmoil of the crypto market and the apparent practices of collateralizing positions in terms of tokens.

These are the conceptual lines that we shall follow in looking at the future monetary panorama, in which stablecoins and central bank digital currency (CBDC) seem to deserve a place. Stablecoins have been conceived so as to solve the price volatility problems that plague cryptocurrencies. In turn, CBDC is meant to provide a safe digital instrument that may enable retail and wholesale trades to exploit the technological advantages of private coins. One even hears about ***programmable*** central bank money. The debates about these new instruments should revolve around the monetary status of stablecoins and the new channels originated by CDBC in the hierarchy of money. It has been decisively affirmed that issuers of stablecoins should be regulated as banks. We shall address these themes in Chapters 5 and 6, building on the insights that we shall develop in Chapter 2 about the different problems of trust that pertain to a blockchain and to the hierarchy of money.

It matters to grasp the monetary problem of trust as a problem of liquidity that differentiates from the computer science of trust that Nakamoto has contributed to evolve. Liquidity is provided by dealers that, for profit, host liquidity risks in their balance sheets. These are mechanisms that decentralized consensus is not in a position to bypass, and that lie at the very foundations of payment systems.

1.3.1 Evolving Digital Payments

The ongoing evolution of digital payments is a relevant dynamic in the monetary arena. Technological advances foster the efficiency and interoperability of different platforms for instantaneous payments, in a competition in which private businesses and governments at times find themselves joining efforts. In such a process, cryptocurrencies and DeFi applications, despite ambitious promises, do not share dominant positions as yet, and can hardly do so in the foreseeable future. A recent special report of The Economist (2023) provides a useful snapshot of the current landscape, in which dominant players have emerged in India and Brazil, and the bank/card model still dominates the scene in the more advanced financial systems.

Over the last few years, the Unified Payment Interface (UPI) in India has acquired a dominant position in the market for instant retail payments. It is sponsored by the government and managed by the National Payments Corporation of India, and charges no fees (obviously, Indian banks complain). The system is not flawless, and customers have developed risk-aversion toward the use of the system for 'large' transactions (say, large in the sense of comparable to monthly wage), and rather use it systematically for transactions of small size. UPI has been linked with Singapore's fast payments system and a number of countries have been invited to join the network, which may become a truly relevant international network for cross-border low-value payments.

Pix is a platform for instant payment developed by Banco Central do Brazil. Launched in November 2020, Pix shares analogies with UPI, in particular, both systems enable direct transfer from one account to another. Pix charges low fees and seems to achieve larger penetration and transaction value (as a ratio to GDP) compared with UPI.

China is another extraordinary scene for the evolution of digital payments. An official digital currency has already been introduced, and the closed duopoly of Alipay and WeChat Pay has been interacting with the government in a story that may well deserve a monograph of its own.

In this global contest, cryptocurrencies and stablecoins can hardly rival the services provided by the aforementioned giants, and, after all, they have not been conceived to intercept the demand for these highly centralized services. One further notes that if crypto faces the same regulation as fintech firms, it is not clear how it can offer anything uniquely valuable. The Economist argues that crypto will not remake the global financial system because it has proved neither efficient nor immune to regulation.

Still, truly interesting case studies are given by the adoption of Bitcoin as the official currency by El Salvador in 2021 and Central African Republic in 2022. Without questioning the motivations of such eccentric policy choices, one notices that the implied instability of exchange rates with other currencies does not fit current global monetary stabilization arrangements. Furthermore, a noticeable departure from international standards of auditable trails stands out. In our view, a decade from now these case studies may provide unique lessons about the way idiosyncratic conditions superpose to universal traits of digital innovations, like the fact that such innovations unleash greater potential in less developed financial systems.

At the end of the report, The Economist (2023) witnesses that the bank/card model is proving remarkably resilient in the advanced economies, and at the same time argues that new digital payments may unleash great potential in the near future, reduce frictions for domestic and cross-border payments, and add value to many economies. Some even wish that new digital arrangements may reduce the global privilege of the US dollar. Interestingly, The Economist notices that no payment system is perfect. "Going cashless also comes with risks. During the pandemic, despite a surge in digital payments, the amount of physical cash in circulation rose, by about 10% in Britain. Part of the reason was a flight to safety. What if banks or critical infrastructure were to go down?" (ivi).

1.3.2 *Physical Cash*

The ICT revolution initiated in the last century is an ongoing tale; the evolution of digital payments represents an important chapter of the story.

In the 1990s real-time internet banking services and online payment gateways were introduced, paving the way for the evolution of credit and debit cards with the EMV (Europay, Visa, Mastercard) standard for chip and PIN. Then came the introduction of virtual wallets and contactless payment, followed by a continuous evolution of mobile payment applications, featuring, in recent years, biometric authentication. One looks at this story of technological advances with admiration.

In this story, the relative decline of the use of physical cash in the advanced economies is a secular phenomenon that central banks are accompanying so as to render it as smooth as possible. For instance, the commitment of the European Central Bank to guarantee freedom of payment choice is explicitly stated in ECB (2022); the central bank aims for the availability of physical cash for day-to-day payments in terms of the working of the infrastructures for the distribution of banknotes and coins. Still, after the advent of blockchain technology, arguments about the desirability of drastic reductions in the use (possibly, a complete elimination) of physical cash are being intermingled with the debates on new digital money. This mixing produces weird logical superpositions that we want to get out of the way of the development of our discussion. In this approach we align with the BIS (2022) prospect on the future monetary system, which does not advocate a diminished role for physical cash.

Well before the crypto revolution, spurious considerations have been advanced concerning the non-traceability of circulating banknotes. It has been affirmed that a drastic reduction of physical cash would be effective in compressing the activities of organized crime—to our knowledge, this thesis has not been adequately accompanied with explanations of why such organizations would find it truly hard to open different channels to transfer funds, perhaps in connection with a restructuring of activities that would yield comparable returns, or the possibility of exploiting their potential for threat or corruption. Furthermore, the link between the non-traceability of payments and the potential for tax evasion has been repeatedly taken as decisive evidence that reducing the use of physical cash would have beneficial effects on tax receipts and government budgets (in Italy this debate is continuously renewed)—again, these considerations have not always been accompanied with a comparative analysis of the many ways officials can detect evasion. Further, the cost of producing new banknotes to replace deteriorated ones has been considered among the benefits resulting from a reduction of the circulation of physical cash. Still, one such cost-benefit analysis should, among other things, account for the marginal cost of operating and upgrading digital infrastructures and guaranteeing safety from attacks, problems that certainly do not impinge on a primitive object like a piece of paper.

These arguments at times reverberate in current discussions on the ongoing evolution of digital payment instruments. Beginners in monetary problems, albeit under the inspiration of Occam's razor, may find it difficult to disentangle the questionable relevance of the above considerations from the truly general challenges facing monetary institutions. Among other things, a major flaw of the above theses is the assumption that a systemic and physiologic phenomenon like the circulation of banknotes may be considered a sound policy lever for addressing specific pathologies like organized crime. By what metrics and counterfactual assumptions should we gauge the success of one such experiment, and for how long? Is there any hope of eradicating crime?

The fact that countries like India are pursuing the objective of decisively shrinking the circulation of physical cash does not imply that physical cash should be considered a medieval instrument that policymakers should strive to eliminate. One reads from Fig. 1.2 that there are Federal Reserve notes available for circulation worth more than two trillion dollars. Vast use of physical cash is well known to take place in Switzerland and Japan. The ECB witnesses commitment to guarantee the availability of physical cash for day-to-day payments. Should we consider these facts as pathologic? The point is that to advocate drastic changes in the circulation of physical cash requires explicit arguments about the way the real economy may adjust so as to maintain the same level and value of transactions, so as not to reallocate resources across sectors. Recall, that the velocity of monetary aggregates can hardly be fixed exogenously.

References

Anderson R., Moore T. (2006). The economics of information security. Science 314, October 27, 610–613.

Andolfatto D., Martin F. M. (2022). The blockhain revolution: decoding digital currencies. Federal Reserve Bank of St. Louis Review 104 (3), 149–165.

Arnosti N., Weinberg S. M. (2019). Bitcoin: a natural oligopoly. Proceedings of the 10th Innovations in Theoretical Computer Science (ITCS).

Bagehot W. (1873). Lombard Street. Scribner, Armstrong and Co.

Benigno G., Rosa C. (2023). The Bitcoin-macro disconnect. Federal Reserve Bank of New York Staff Report No. 1052.

Biais B., Bisière C., Bouvard M., Casamatta C. (2019). The blockchain folk theorem. Review of Financial Studies 32 (5), 1662–1715.

Biais B., Bisière C., Bouvard M., Casamatta C., Menkveld A. J. (2023). Equilibrium Bitcoin pricing. Journal of Finance 78 (2), 967–1014.

Binmore K. (2007). Playing for Real. Oxford University Press.

BIS (Bank for International Settlements, 2022). The future monetary system. Annual Economic Report.

Budish E. (2018). The economic limits of Bitcoin and the blockchain. NBER Working Paper 24717.

Carstens A. (2019). The future of money and the payment system: what role for central banks? Princeton University Lecture. December.

Catalini C., Gans J. (2020). Some simple economics of the blockchain. Communications of the ACM 63 (7), 80–90.

Chiu J., Koeppl T. (2017). The economics of cryptocurrencies—Bitcoin and beyond.

Davidson M. (2023). State machine replication and consensus with Byzantine adversaries. NIST Internal Report 8460 ipd.

Diamond D., Dybvig P. H. (1983). Bank runs, deposit insurance, and liquidity. Journal of Political Economy 91 (3), 401–419.

ECB (European Central Bank, 2022). Guaranteeing freedom of payment choice: access to cash in the euro area. Economic Bullettin, Issue 5.

Halaburda H., Haeringer G., Gans J., Gandal N. (2022). The microeconomics of cryptocurrencies. Journal of Economic Literature 60 (3), 971–1013.

Kroll J. A., Davey I. C., Felten E. W. (2013). The economics of Bitcoin mining, or Bitcoin in the presence of adversaries. Proceedings of WEIS.

Leshno J. D., Strack P. (2020). Bitcoin: an axiomatic approach and an impossibility theorem. American Economic Review: Insights 2 (3), 269–286.

Mantovi A. (2021). Bitcoin selection rule and foundational game theoretic representation of mining competition. Working Paper. Dipartimento di Scienze Economiche e Aziendali. Parma, Italy.

Nakamoto S. (2008). Bitcoin: a peer-to-peer electronic cash system.

Narayanan A., Bonneau J., Felten E., Miller A., Goldfeder S. (2016). Bitcoin and Cryptocurrency Technologies. Princeton University Press.

Szalay E. (2021). China's crypto crackdown delivers windfall to global bitcoin miners. Financial Times, August 24.

Szidarovszky F., Okuguchi K. (1997). On the existence and uniqueness of pure Nash equilibrium in rent-seeking games. Games and Economic Behavior 18, 135–140.

The Economist (2023). Cashless talk. Special report. May 20th.

CHAPTER 2

Blockchain, Decentralized Consensus, and Trust

Abstract This chapter sets the stage for comparing the problems of trust raised by standard and new money instruments. The computer science of blockchain is summarized in a brief discussion of hashing, time-stamping digital documents and consensus. Our simplified approach to these highly sophisticated issues is meant to fit our economic perspective. The principle of "no questions asked" is taken as the foundation of monetary economics. The problem of safe assets and collateralization is acknowledged as the monetary problem of the millennium. The hierarchy of account-based money is discussed. Bank runs and financial stability as depicted by Diamond and Dybvig are given due emphasis. Finally, we compare the different problems of trust that blockchain solutions and monetary institutions are meant to face. An Appendix argues that classical debates in monetary thinking can have a firm grip on the current evolution of digital money.

Keyword Trust · Blockchain · No questions asked · Hierarchy of money · Bank run

A. Schianchi and A. Mantovi, *The Economics of Cryptocurrencies and Digital Money*, Palgrave Studies in Financial Services Technology, https://doi.org/10.1007/978-3-031-44248-3_2

In this chapter we develop the themes introduced in the previous one. Section 2.1 provides a brief sketch of blockchain architecture as an introduction to the relevance of time-stamping digital data for the immutability of records, and the role of cryptography and PoW in the ecology of a cryptocurrency. Computer scientists may find our discussion somewhat trivial. In fact, computer scientists should skip this section, not to develop a wrong attitude toward the mission of economists of stylizing problems and lines of reasoning. In turn, readers primarily interested in the economics of blockchain should consider Sect. 2.1 simply as guide and stimulus for further study.

Industrial economists are not required to master the chemistry and engineering of industrial production, and still may have incentives to do so. Correspondingly, monetary economists are not required to master the computer science of blockchain, and it is far from obvious what the minimal background in distributed systems and decentralized consensus should be. With no ambition to solve the riddle, the essential aim of this chapter is to set the stage for comparing the problem of trust that blockchain solutions are supposed to overcome with the monetary problem of trust that afflicts new digital coins and worries policymakers and regulators. In this respect, Sect. 2.2 develops the principle of "no questions asked" as the foundation of monetary economics, and then reviews the hierarchy of money and the mechanism at the foundations of financial stability. We thereby introduce the monetary problem of the 2020s, namely, the global problem of safe assets and liquidity that we inherit from the great financial crisis.

The etymology of *crypto* points at the greek κρυπτός, that means hidden, or secret. The history of cryptology (that initiates centuries before Christ) stages heterogeneous traditions and characters, among whom some of the founding fathers of computer science like Charles Babbage and Alan Turing.[1] To a large extent, it is a history of hiding the content of messages, i.e. a history of encryption, decryption and proper interpretation of messages. However, in this chapter we shall be dealing with the authentication of digital data, that represents a recent entry in the history

[1] Alan Turing is not only a giant of cryptology, but a giant of mathematics in the broader sense. One can simply recall his pathbreaking contributions to formal systems and decidability. Kurt Gödel made fundamental use of Turing's ideas. See the article by Copeland and Fan in the *Mathematical Intelligencer* 44 (4), 2022.

of mankind; at stake shall not be the proper deciphering of messages but the integrity of data. Let us recall a few definitions.

Cryptology is the study of secrecy systems. *Cryptography* deals with the design and implementation of secrecy systems; *cryptoanalysis* deals with deciphering and breaking codes. The astonishing rate at which computational resources have become increasingly available over the last decades has magnified the relevance and applicability of cryptography and cybersecurity. The Nakamoto design marks a further step in this history, as an alleged solution to the problem of double-spending digital cash. Part of the public may also associate the term *crypto* with the kind of "anonymity" that is connected with evading authentication of identity, eluding regulation, avoiding prosecutability and perhaps engaging in illegal activity. This interpretation may well represent a further layer of complexity in our discussion.

2.1 Blockchain and Decentralized Consensus

A blockchain is a shared digital record-keeping system encompassing a mechanism that enables participants to agree at regular intervals on the true state of the shared data. A precise definition goes as follows. A blockchain is a distributed digital ledger of cryptographically signed transactions that are grouped into blocks. Each block is cryptographically linked to the previous one (making it tamper evident) after validation and undergoing a consensus decision. As new blocks are added, older blocks become more difficult to modify (creating tamper resistance). New blocks are replicated across copies of the ledger within the network, and any conflicts are resolved automatically using established rules. However, it has been pointed out that such a definition may fail to envision a blockchain as a particular data structure within a broader set of distributed ledgers (Davidson, 2023). For sure, hashing is at the core of the architecture.

2.1.1 Hashing and Proof-of-Work

A *perfect hash function* is an injective function that maps an input string (a *message*) of a definite type into an output string of another (possibly the same) type, such that the inverse function is not computable. Concretely existing hash functions are algorithms that target this ideal of perfection. The expressions *with no collisions* and *collision-free* are often used to denote the injectivity of a hash function, and are motivated by the concrete operations into which these functions are involved. A prominent example is the Secure Hash Algorithm (SHA) family, developed by the US National Security Agency, whose elements map strings of arbitrary type into strings of hexadecimal characters (the 16 characters encompassing the ten digits and the first six letters). In particular, the output of the function SHA-256 employed by the Bitcoin blockchain is a string of 64 characters like 8A21 38DD 3B3A 6511 863C 92D4 92C5 7126 ABAD 437E E1F2 5B22 99D1 1A5B 7278 A00A, that looks like a random (in the sense of apparent lack of recognizable patterns) sequence of hexadecimals. This apparent randomness is connected with the scope of a hash function.

Direct computational exploration reveals that a slight change in the input string of these functions results in a dramatic change in output. The reason for this occurrence is the crucial feature that a hash function is meant to share, namely, it must be hard (in some well specified sense) to identify the "unique" input that yields a definite output. As a consequence, brute force methods (typically, the ergodic exploration of the space of potential solutions) are the only systematic approach that one can employ to achieve this goal. In fact, explicit hash functions may not be injective: if both domain and range are finite, and if domain is larger than range, injectivity is evidently ruled out.[2] What matters is the practical impossibility to solve the inversion problem; in this respect, the size of the domain is crucial.

In a sense, hash functions can be considered encryption devices but is matters to recall that encryption is typically employed for safeguarding the secrecy of a message that is supposed to be transmitted and subsequently deciphered by someone in possession of the proper cipher. On the other hand, the role of hashing in blockchain operation has to do with authentication. For sure, the properties of a hash function make it useful for cryptographic purposes, and hash functions are among the key cryptographic primitives, together with pseudorandom generators and signature schemes. In the nascent jargon of blockchain the term *hash* is

[2] It has been a great achievement of Georg Cantor to establish that a set can be made in a 1-1 correspondence with a proper subset if and only if it is infinite, and that bijections can be used to define a hierarchy of cardinality for both finite and infinite sets. The solvability of the Continuum Hypothesis (the nonexistence of an intermediate cardinality between integers and real numbers) is still an active area of research.

used to denote different aspects of the process of block validation: the noun *hash* is used to denote the solution of the cryptopuzzle, the verb *hashing* has become synonymous of mining; to *reverse hash* denotes the inverse operation of hashing. Familiarity with the way terms are used can be useful.

The computer science of PoW dates at least to the 1990s, when researchers have been uncovering the theoretical relevance for cryptographic purposes that some agents demonstrate of having performed a certain amount of computational task. For the Nakamoto design, a brute force computational task is meant to identify the *nonce* (an expression that some interpret as abbreviation of number used once) to be time-stamped on the block under validation (see Fig. 2.1). In this context, PoW is often referred to as "hashing to guess the nonce." A hash inequality with a definite number of initial zeroes gauges the difficulty of the puzzle; one writes

$$H\left(\text{nonce}\middle|\ \text{prev\_hash}|tx|tx\middle|\ldots|tx\right) < \text{target}$$

(see Narayanan et al., 2016, p. 41).

Hashing the function SHA-256 is a highly specific task for which general purpose processing units have been progressively substituted with hardware with increasing specialization, from graphics processing units, to field programmable gate arrays and, finally, application specific integrated circuit (ASIC); see Narayanan et al. (2016) for an account of this process in connection with the specificities of computing SHA-256. Economists may find it intriguing to deepen this theme, still, from an economic standpoint, the relevant degree of freedom is the increase in competitiveness in the transition from one type of hardware to another; such competitiveness unfolds in a twofold guise. On the one hand, it enhances the speed of computational effort, and therefore increases the probability of

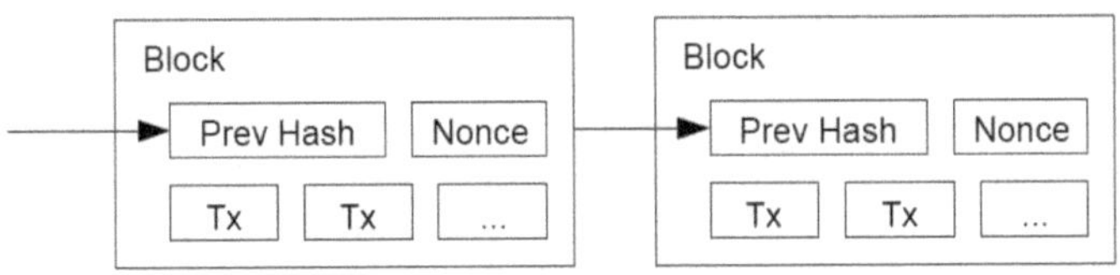

Fig. 2.1 The time-stamping of blocks as the chain develops. Reproduced from Nakamoto (2008)

winning rewards; on the other hand, it reduces costs. In the language of Sect. 1.2, the former aspect pertains to the "effective" level of activity that a miner achieves in the selection rule, and that results in the increase in expected reward, whereas the latter concerns the cost competitiveness, and therefore the entry threshold, which differentiates miners.

True, the wasted resources involved in PoW make economists instinctively think of sunk costs, commitment, and intermingled incentives through which to explore the conceptual space of strategic mining. In this panorama the problem of trust does not emerge in its pure form. It is therefore important for economists to sharpen the sense in which a problem of "trust" is at the foundations of the computer science of blockchain, beginning with the problem of time-stamping a digital document.

2.1.2 Time-Stamping

In a beautiful short paper, Stuart Haber and Scott Stornetta (1991) address the criticalities connected with the authentication of digital documents. Problems are generated from the fact that digital documents are easy to tamper with without leaving telltale signs. The Authors envision ways to solve this problem in terms of time-stamping the data, not the physical medium. The authentication of intellectual property is an intuitive setting for grasping the essence of the problem.

One such intellectual property may not be in serious dispute once a physical medium is available as record of the date at which a patentable idea has been written down, and a *trusted* authority further guarantees the integrity of the record. It has been the achievement of Haber and Stornetta to set the framework for the development of time-stamping as a solution to the problem of authentication of digital records in the absence of a trusted authority. Readers are referred to the original paper for a satisfactory discussion; the following brief sketch of the paper is simply meant to set the scene for comparing the different forms of trust addressed by Nakamoto and central bankers.

The building blocks of the problem encompass in first instance a "time-stamping service" (TSS) in charge of authenticating the date a document was created. One such service may be subject to problems of security, incompetence and/or dubious trustworthiness. A second assumption is the existence of reliable digital signatures that uniquely identify the sender of a communication. Given this assumption, once an agent submits a request for authentication to the TSS, the service processes the request and responds by sending a signed certificate to the agent, thereby establishing certainty that the request has been (perhaps correctly) processed. Agents are assumed to be uniquely identified by identification numbers.

Further building blocks of the discussion are hash functions. One such function can be used to encrypt the digital document that one wants to authenticate, and thereby keep its content secret. One can then require authentication of this hashed document, since authentication of the hashed version is equivalent to the authentication of the original document. Hash functions, in conjunction with signatures, solve part of the problems of the TSS, and one is left with the problem of the trustworthiness of the TSS, for which Haber and Stornetta design a pair of approaches. "The first approach is to constrain a centralized but possibly untrustworthy TSS to produce genuine time-stamps in such a way that fake ones are difficult to produce. The second approach is somehow to distribute the required trust among the users of the service" (ivi). The spirit of both solutions inspires the Nakamoto design.

The first approach builds on a *linking* procedure in which the TSS is necessary. The key insight is that the history of past records provides evidence that the new document is more recent (and this mechanism can constrain the date even in the future direction). Essential to the method is the use of a hash function by the TSS, in addition to the use of other hash functions by clients. Once a client submits a request of time-stamping, the TSS responds by sending the client a signed certificate of the request encompassing a link to the previously issued certificate. Subsequently, when the next request is submitted, the TSS sends the same above client the identification number of this new request. The resulting chain of records is hard to alter, the only way being to prepare a fake chain of time-stamps, long enough to satisfy the most suspicious challenger. One can already envision some analogy with the "immutability" of the chain of blocks that characterizes the Nakamoto design.

The second approach entails a *decentralized* information processing connected with the use of a reliable pseudorandom generator, and a TSS is not necessary. A client builds a hash of the document to be time-stamped, and then uses this hash as seed for the pseudorandom generator, which returns an output that is interpreted as a *k*-tuple of client identification numbers. The client sends requests for authentication to each of these clients, and each of them returns a signed message including a time-stamp. The desired time-stamp then coincides with the combination of the initial hash with the sequence of signatures and times returned by other clients. The only way to alter this time-stamping is to use an initial hash value that identifies *k* clients willing to collude in altering the record, but there are evident limits to this possibility, connected with both the randomness of *k*-tuple generated by the algorithm and the fraction of potentially dishonest nodes.

The two above approaches differ in the way dates are made impossible to alter but entail similar assumptions concerning the specification of the security level attained by a solution. For instance, assumptions must be explicitly stated about the amount of computational resources distributed in the environment, that may challenge the robustness of the above hashing scheme (much like a "51% attack" may endanger a PoW blockchain).

Needless to say, the above short discussion makes no justice of the achievements of Haber and Stornetta, and still may help readers refine intuitions about the relevance of time-stamping digital data and the role of cryptography therein. In particular, it matters for economists to appreciate what kind of "trust" is at stake in the problem of time-stamping, as a first step toward the elaboration of the difference with the monetary problem of trust in a payment instrument. Haber and Strornetta face the problem of trust in the TSS that is called to authenticate the date a document was created. This kind of trust is located at a specific degree of freedom (the TSS), and concerns the option space available to the TSS for *intentional* misbehavior. On the other hand, trust in a monetary instrument is a distributed collection of self-reinforcing beliefs that, in principle, has nothing to do with misbehavior: one must recall that a bank is potentially subject to runs even if it is perfectly healthy (we shall elaborate on this).

Finally, we are in a position to appreciate the relevance of time-stamping in the Nakamoto (2008) design as "solution to the double-spending problem using a peer-to-peer distributed timestamp server to generate computational proof of the chronological order of transactions" (ivi). Recall the six steps of the flowchart identified by the Bitcoin protocol.

> First, new transactions are broadcast to the nodes.
> Second, each node collects new transactions into a block.
> Third, each node works on finding a difficult PoW for its block.

Fourth, when a node finds a PoW, it broadcasts the block to all nodes.
Fifth, nodes accept the block only if all transactions in it are valid.
Sixth, nodes express their acceptance by working on creating the next block in the chain, using the hash of the last accepted block as the previous hash.

The role of time-stamps in this flowchart is essential: the complete set of nodes plays the role of the TSS. Blocks (the digital data under concern) are time-stamped with hash values, and each time-stamp contains the previous time-stamp in its hash, so that a continuously developing chain of blocks provides the record-keeping of validated transactions as in the figure below.

This blockchain is "append-only," in that a newly validated block is supposed to be appended to the last previously hashed block, so as to prolong a well ordered chain of blocks. This logic is fixed in the "longest chain rule" (LCR) that represents as an essential part of the Nakamoto design (as is well known, deviations from the rule have manifested, witness the number of forks that have occurred in the Bitcoin chain). The LCR is connected with the crucial role of majority in the Nakamoto philosophy; in the words of Nakamoto (2008) himself: "The longest chain serves not only as a proof of the sequence of events, but proof that it came from the largest pool of CPU power. As long as a majority of CPU power is controlled by nodes that are not cooperating to attack the network, they'll generate the longest chain and outpace attackers." Thus, Nakamoto himself points at a weakness of his design, and a large number of papers have been devoted to the majority problem and its elaborations, as a problem of incentive compatibility of the protocol.

Our technical sketch of blockchain design proceeds with a few hints on the computer science of decentralized consensus.

2.1.3 Decentralized Consensus

Social scientists may be free to use the terms *agreement* and *consensus* with the standard significance of ordinary language. Computer scientists, on the other hand, have developed interpretations of these terms that monetary economists may want to grasp to some extent, eventually building some intuition on problems of security in general computer science, and in particular within a blockchain. "Having been deployed in Bitcoin since

January 2009, Nakamoto consensus has the most real-world battle testing of any permissionless protocol" (Davidson, 2023, p. 107). "Bitcoin works better in practice than in theory [...] only when we have a strong theoretical understanding of how Bitcoin consensus works will we have strong guarantees of Bitcoin's security and stability" (Narayanan et al., 2016, pp. 31–32). Under the inspiration of these quotes, we shall sketch a few traits of the drama of liveness and safety in the presence of adversaries.

The limited size of this subsection prevents us from even stating precise definitions of concepts, and the sense of this subsection resembles a trailer of a motion picture, showing the characters at play and a sketch of the plot. To enjoy the complete story, economists can find a clear logic of development in the lessons on the foundations of blockchains by Tim Roughgarden, available online, in the articles by Lewis-Pye and Roughgarden (2021, 2023), available on arXiv, and in the report by Michael Davidson (2023). Economists might enjoy coming to grips with the endogenous phenomena at play in a distributed system, and perhaps envision some connection with the celebrated problem of *agreeing to disagree* (Aumann, 1982).

At the conceptual foundations of distributed systems one acknowledges the problem of fault tolerance. When a task is distributed among a set of nodes, part of the nodes may not perform or communicate correctly, and possibly compromise the working of the system. The tolerance of the system to such faults is crucial for the usefulness itself of the system, and a massive body of theory of distributed computing and distributed system design has grown over the decades. Fault tolerance can be considered the flip side of the usefulness of replicating data and functions across a network of nodes in order to avoid single point of failure.

To begin with, one distinguishes technical problems of crash fault from malicious attacks in which human choice is at play. Malicious nodes have been represented as Byzantine generals by Leslie Lamport, Robert Shostak and Marshall Pease in a celebrated article published in 1982 (curiously, the same year of publication of Aumann's *Agreeing to disagree*). The metaphor goes that a number of Byzantine generals commanded legions camped around a fortress under siege. Generals can devise plans for attack but can communicate only via messengers that are not reliable, as a metaphor of technical problems. Part of the generals as well are not reliable; these generals may have incentives not to reach agreement on plans of attack or pretend not to have been alerted, perhaps to evade the fight or because they are traitors.

This metaphor has inspired the development of the theory of consensus for *permissioned* systems, i.e. distributed systems in which the set of nodes is fixed and known at the outset, each node being properly identified. Unsurprisingly, problems of broadcast and agreement in the presence of malicious nodes have been attracting increasing interest with the advent of the Internet and have been referred to as *Byzantine broadcast* and *Byzantine agreement*. On the other hand, the recent introduction of Bitcoin embodies the paradigm of *permissionless* consensus as part of the egalitarian philosophy of freedom from a central authority. In such a setting, the number of participant nodes is not fixed, Sybil identities can be created at will, entry needs no permission, and incumbent nodes can stop (perhaps temporarily) operations. This innovative architecture opens uncharted territory for the computer science of decentralized consensus, and researchers are actively engaged in extending the established theory to the new landscape.

Decentralized consensus in the Bitcoin platform can be defined as follows (Narayanan et al., 2016): given a set of nodes, each with an input value, and a subset of faulty or malicious nodes, a distributed consensus protocol (I) must terminate with all honest nodes in agreement on the value (*agreement*), and (II) the value must have been generated by an honest node (*validity*). Properties (I) and (II) are basic traits of the drama that we want to put in perspective, beyond the crucial role of randomization in PoW consensus. Let us recall a few definitions.

A distributed system model is *synchronous* if it admits a shared global clock and a known upper bound on massage delay. If neither assumption holds, the system model is *asynchronous*. The former model shares ideal features (it allows failures to be detected by simply waiting an entire time step for a reply, and assuming a crash has happened if no response arrives) but is overly demanding (outages are ruled out), and some of its properties are not desirable (a synchronous system does not tolerate network partitions). The latter model is overly relaxed, and its properties are scarcely satisfactory. In between these opposite benchmark models one can define a more realistic *partially synchronous* model as one in which both synchronous and asynchronous phases can occur, a shared global clock exists, and the asynchronous phase is characterized by a *global stabilization time* (GST), after which a known upper bound exists on message delay. With these notions in place, one can define safety properties stating that "something wrong" never happens, and liveness properties stating that "something useful" can happen, eventually, after the GST.

It is an educated guess that the more realistic partially synchronous model can provide an appropriate description of the working of a blockchain. For sure, Roughgarden places decisive emphasis on a "big result" that economists may be willing to acknowledge (and perhaps enroll in the economics of information) concerning the "magical threshold" 1/3 that features in a number of white papers on blockchain consensus: in a partially synchronous model there exists a deterministic protocol for the Byzantine agreement problem that satisfies agreement, validity and eventual liveness (post-GTS) if and only if the fraction of faulty or malicious nodes is strictly below 1/3.

Further basic notions. The Public Key Infrastructure (PKI) is the assumption that nodes know each other's public keys and therefore are in a position to verify signatures. State Machine Replication (SMR) is a theoretical framework introduced by Leslie Lamport for discussing the way a fault tolerant system can emulate a centralized one. The framework encompasses input variables, states, a transition function that takes input and state and returns a new state, and an output function that takes input and state and returns an output. The key idea is to focus on the order of operations, so that transactions operate on some global state and perform deterministic transformations that maintain lock-step execution of identical commands and agreement on the state by all honest processes. This approach has shaped a number of classical protocols addressing Byzantine agreement for permissioned systems.

Much of the theory of distributed systems concerns possibility ("positive") and impossibility ("negative") results. In a celebrated article, Fisher et al. (1985, "FLP") established that an asynchronous network of computing nodes with an initial value is not in a position to solve the problem of consensus as the combination of agreement, validity and *termination*, i.e. the property that all non-faulty processes decide on a value. This result establishes a fundamental conceptual benchmark; on the other hand, this theoretical impossibility does not preclude the factual well functioning of concrete systems, that, typically, do not satisfy the FLP assumptions.

The flavor of the FLP result compares to the Consistency Availability Partition tolerance (CAP) principle, according to which only two of the three informal properties can be attained in a distributed system. Consistency means that the performance of the distributed system is indistinguishable from that of a centralized one, a property that compares to safety. Availability means that all requests from clients are processed, a requirement that compares to the liveness of the system. Partition tolerance means that the above properties should hold even in case the system partitions, for instance under a denial-of-service attack. The tradeoff involved in the CAP principle compares to the FLP result, in that in an attack (an asynchronous phase or a partition) one either sacrifices liveness/availability or safety/consistency. However, FLP impossibility constrains asynchronous systems only, whereas CAP impossibility holds in every system. According to Roughgarden, CAP impossibility is easier to establish since messages can be delayed forever in the CAP setting, so that the adversary is potentially more powerful that in the FLP setting and making impossibility easier to establish.

Current research aims at extending the theory of distributed systems to the recent designs of blockchain architectures; first and foremost, this is a quest for the fundamental degrees of freedom. Well, the new landscape stages a key role for resources (see Lewis-Pye and Roughgarden, 2021). A protocol targets a scarce resource, and then selects identifiers as a function of their resource balances. One starts with a resource pool as a function that allocates a resource balance to each participant. Then, one allows processors to make request to a *permitter oracle*, which establishes the possibility to broadcast a new block as a function of the individual balance. For Bitcoin, the permitter oracle gives a positive response with a probability that depends on the hashrate, according to the Bitcoin selection rule (our game theoretic discussion of this rule can be considered an economic perspective on this theme). Oracles are a standard concept in cryptography literature that in the evolving panorama displays renewed relevance.

Thus, players are characterized by balances of resources (hashrate for PoW, stakes for PoS) that trigger the possibility to propose updates of the state of the system. In turn, adversaries are characterized by bounds on the fraction of global resources that they can deploy. Then, a major concern is to represent the way the resource pool informs the properties of the protocol. In this respect one defines *sized* and *unsized* settings. A *sized* setting is one in which the resource pool is a protocol input; PoS is a naturally described in this setting. An *unsized* setting, on the contrary, is such that the resource pool is unknown; PoW is naturally represented as unsized, since the dynamics of individual hashrates is not given ex ante.

Given these premises, Lewis-Pye and Roughgarden (2023) tailor elements of a map of the new terrain that computer scientists are called to cover. Intuition suggests that PoS, so to say, requires "more permission" than PoW. Well, the Authors define a hierarchy of grades of "permissionlessness" that gauge the departure from the classical permissioned setting. A *fully permissionless setting* is one in which the protocol has no knowledge about current participation; this is the natural setting for discussing PoW protocols. A *dynamically available setting* is one in which the protocol knows a dynamic list of identifiers, and active nodes are a subset of this list; longest chain PoS protocols are naturally represented in this setting. A *quasi-permissionless setting* is a special case of the previous setting in which all nodes are active; BFT-style PoS protocols are naturally described in this way. Along this hierarchy, evidently, the more permissionlessness, the less the hope of establishing positive results. In the fully permissionless setting, even with the synchronous assumption and severe restrictions on the number of Byzantine players, the Authors find that every deterministic protocol that solves the Byzantine agreement problem has infinite execution.

We refer to the recent articles by Lewis-Pye and Roughgarden for a truly engaging account of these stimulating research advances, whose aim is to tailor a homogeneous theoretical framework for extending well established lines of reasoning and results to the permissionless setting. Davidson (2023) in particular provides a thorough discussion of the way the SMR concept displays a decisive role in this evolving theoretical scenario.

The content of this subsection may provide economists with a preliminary view of the fuzzy boundary between the economics and the computer science of blockchain, so as to refine intuitions about the generality of recent results on the security of a blockchain network as an economic outcome, for which Pagnotta (2022) provides an insightful discussion. The process of maintaining the ledger must generate incentives enough to attract validators, and the security of a blockchain depends on the number of resources dedicated to it. That being the case, the precise analytical characterization of the mining game is crucial for both the computer science and the economics of PoW, in which the global hashrate emerges as the pivotal degree of freedom (again, see Pagnotta, 2022).

2.1.4 *Miners and Pools*

The nature and objectives of the Bitcoin enterprise is decentralized in manifold ways. One of these ways unfolds through the self-selection of participants. In particular, the Nakamoto design concerns the incentives for miners to enter the scene.

Potential miners are attracted by reward prospects, and effectively self-appoint themselves as miners once profit and risk prospects seem to fit one's risk-attitude. The key innovation of the Nakamoto design is to embed *strategic* incentives in the computer science of decentralized consensus: the incentives that attract miners do interact, in that the Bitcoin protocol posits a PoW competition among miners for the authentication of transactions. In turn, mining activity results in the minting of new coins—the expression "monetary policy" has been used for this mechanism. This incentive design should lead miners to behave honestly, since rewards are valid only if their records are endorsed by other miners.

The form of the competition among miners is a rent-seeking contest that game theorists have been studying at least since the 1980s. The conceptual relevance of such form of competition has been the intuition of Gordon Tullock, that in the late 1960s initiated a systematic inquiry of rent-seeking in the economics of public choice. We are not told whether "Nakamoto"—whoever the pseudonym refers to—had in mind Tullock contests as the strategic dimension of Bitcoin; however, it is a plain fact that the literature converges in looking at the essence of Bitcoin mining in such terms.

The objectives of game theoretic analysis are manifold, and do not reduce to the "explanation" (in some sense) of empirical evidence. Among other things, researchers have been discussing the logical consistency itself of the Bitcoin protocol, i.e. the compatibility of the strategic design in Nakamoto (2008) with the objectives of decentralization of the underlying philosophy. The final word on these matters may be hard to fix, but the inquiry proceeds at a rapid pace.

We have already seen in the previous chapter (Sect. 1.2) that the basic one-shot mining competition is shaped by the selection rule (contest success function) and by the distribution of cost competitiveness among miners. At more refined levels of description one can represent the indefinite repetition of the game, and then the differentiation of players, in primis between miners and users, and further introducing hardware producers, pool managers, etc. However, all of these developments build on the analytical foundation the Bitcoin selection rule

$$p_i(x) = \frac{x^i}{\sum_{j=1}^{n} x^j} \equiv \frac{x^i}{s(x)}$$

In this formula, the variables x^i represent the amount of computational effort exerted by miners. According to this rule, the probability p_i with which miner i turns out to be the winner of the contest is the share of overall computational resources deployed by the miner himself. The unique winner of the contest makes profits, provided reward exceeds costs; all other miners make losses. The term "lottery" is often used to denote the probabilistic character of this rule. The aggregate variable s is the pivot of this logic.

In fact, the Bitcoin selection rule is characterized by the analytical form of the denominator of the RHS of the formula, namely, the *aggregate* activity of miners, that we write s. This property has the relevant consequence that, formally, each miner can be considered to respond to s in his strategic reasoning. Information about who does what is simply irrelevant at this level of description. In this sense, the reduction of anonymity to the symmetry of the game envisioned by Leshno and Strack (2020) can be considered a sound economic step (that, though, may sound strange or disappointing to computer scientists).

The global hashrate is a sound gauge of the aggregate activity s, provided one assumes that miners are homogeneous with respect to hardware performance. The literature is progressively uncovering the sense in which the global hashrate is the pivotal degree of freedom of the problem. for instance, in a setting in which individual miners can allocate their resources in different mining pools, Cong et al. (2021) advocate a decomposition of the global hashrate into active and passive components, the former component representing computational resources deployed strategically, namely, contingent on the fees charged by pools. The latter component represents the part of the allocation of resources that is not subject to strategic behavior.

We find it stimulating to return to the metaphor of chess for introducing the game theoretic inquiry on PoW. The Bitcoin protocol fixes the rules of the mining game, but the complexity of the problem makes it impossible to anticipate what the emergent phenomena will turn out to be. In much the same way, the theory of chess is a systematic account of what players, over the centuries, have experienced in their exploration of the strategic space of the game. It is noticeable that computer scientists and economists display a consensus on the fact that the most interesting phenomenology of PoW concerns the way decentralization manifest itself in its empirical connection with concentration in mining. The emerging concentration in mining is a plain fact. It has been argued that this occurrence represents an empirical rejection of the Nakamoto philosophy; however, in order to shape rigorous lines of argument on these matters, one can hardly avoid use of explicit model games.

Researches are actively engaged in discussing the way economies of scale and scope in mining are intermingled. A significant perspective on the concentration of mining concerns the vertical structure of the industry. In Chapter 4 we shall review a model by Arnosti and Weinberg (2022) of a two-stage model game of mining activity and hardware production. The model displays equilibria that rationalize vertical concentration in the industry, therefore shedding light on the naturalness of such a vertical structure; in the model, both the differentiation of cost competitiveness and the price competition in the sale of hardware contribute to the concentration of mining, at the expense of decentralization.

Capponi et al. (2021) represent an analogous picture of the vertical structure of the industry, in which miners invest in state-of-the art hardware in order to enhance their competitiveness, and face capacity constraints (vertical integration is not considered). The Authors, in line with Arnosti and Weinberg, notice that heterogeneous cost competitiveness fosters centralization in mining (recall our discussion in Sect. 1.2); however, the presence of capacity constraints counters the positive interaction of investment and cost competitiveness.

True, the emergence of mining pools may represent the *key* structural change that PoW ecologies have been experiencing in their short history. A substantial consensus rationalizes the emergence of pools for risk sharing purposes. Ideal risk-neutral miners have no incentives to conglomerate, whereas real miners are typically risk-averse, and find it useful to share risks and smooth profit prospects, if only for liquidity purposes. Well, pools provide one such liquidity service, in that miners can contract claims on average reward that are paid on a regular basis. In Chapter 4 we shall review the model of Cong et al. (2021) of the strategic interaction of miners and pool managers. In the model pools share market power, that manifests itself in the fee setting policy. Interestingly, the model displays endogenous forces that mean-revert the growth momentum of pools, and therefore prevent overconcentration in the hands of a single pool.

As already pointed out, our aim is not a comprehensive review of the extant literature on cryptocurrencies and blockchain ecology; rather, we aim at building a *vision* on the literature in terms of sharp intuitions about the strategic forces at play in a PoW arena like Bitcoin. An explicit analysis of representative models, albeit in a qualitative and synthetic approach, is an unavoidable step of the journey. This is one of the key lessons of game theory (and, one may say, of economics in general): one needs an explicit model in order to fix what strategies are in place and what payoffs are at stake. To interpret the advent and evolution of pools is essentially a strategic problem, that is to a large extent disconnected from specific technological aspects.

We shall find that the basic mining game introduced in Sect. 1.2 is a sound guide along this tour, that enables one to envision the global hashrate as the pivotal degree of freedom at play. This does not mean that it is the *cause* of phenomena; rather, the point is the pivotal analytical role played in equilibrium conditions. One envisions the Nash equilibrium of the basic mining game as an essential part of the more elaborated equilibria of more articulated games. On top of that, recall that one is not in search of the "right" model of mining competition, in the same sense in which economists are not in search of the right model of industrial competition.

2.1.5 Proof-of-Stake

A major drawback of PoW is the wasteful nature of mining competition. The continuing increase of the Bitcoin global hashrate has resulted in huge consumption of electric energy; recent estimates revolve around an order of magnitude that compares with the yearly consumption of a country like Norway. The conception of the Proof-of-Stake (PoS) paradigm seems to have been largely inspired by the desire to fix this wasteful property of PoW.

The idea of substituting PoW with a voting mechanism based on token ownership is reported to have appeared in the blog bitcointalk.org in July 2011. However, Sunny King is credited the conception of PoS. The design has been released in a white paper with Scott Nadal of 2012 in which a hybrid PoS-PoW protocol is described. The protocol has been subsequently adopted as stand-alone; to date, a few dozen blockchain seem to implement this protocol.

In its essential conception, PoS tailor the privilege to validate blocks as connected with "stakes" of coins. A node engaged in validation (a "forger") places this stakes in a specific wallet that temporarily freezes these funds. A stochastic assignment of the privilege then results in a larger fraction of block validated by forgers that stake higher. This mechanism does not entail the brute force computational power of hashing SHA-256 and is considered more "fair" that the one underlying Bitcoin. However, the weaknesses of this picture have been pointed out. Among other things, the incentives to hoard coins may counter the use of coins as means of exchange and promote the emergence of a dominating elite of forgers.

One further acknowledges the problem of "Nothing-at-Stake," that has been raised concerning the resolution of a fork. One considers the incentives of forgers to append a block, and notices that to append is weakly dominant strategy whatever the breach involved. This problem is currently a matter of debate.

In September 2022 the Ethereum system has switched to PoS, and this case study will provide decisive empirical evidence on the nature of PoS. As expected, a game theoretic inquiry of PoS is emerging. Also emerging is a variety of paradigms like Proof-of-Activity, Proof-of-Capacity, Proof-of-Weight, that within a few years may manifest their effectiveness in concrete large-scale applications.

2.2 Trust

2.2.1 No Questions Asked

It has been argued that DeFi may generate more inclusive and transparent financial services. The relevance of such a technological possibility is beyond question, but in the transition from a technological possibility to an economic reality one may face problems. For sure, transparency comes at the cost of *information sensitivity*. It may seem puzzling that researchers are still grappling with the implications of this intuitive fact. Well, this is indeed the case. And is a case of rethinking the foundations themselves of the theory of financial markets. A major contribution to this effort is given by Bengt Holmström (2015), that sheds new light on the differences between stock markets and money markets. These markets can be taken as polar opposites with respect to the role of information processing.

At one extreme one finds stock markets, in which prices are extremely sensitive to information. The stock market itself can be considered a sophisticated information processing mechanism for the pricing of risk, in which participants engage in refining assessments of the riskiness of businesses, and continuously renew a "decentralized consensus" on varying market prices. In so doing, market participants are also uncovering the demand of investors for the risk profiles floating in the different exchanges around the world. This well-known mechanism goes hand in hand with the fact that large listed companies at the technological frontier (think of Google) are largely or completely equity-financed.

At the other extreme one finds debt markets and money markets, in which one wants no questions asked on the value and sustainability of positions. Historians have convincingly pointed out the relevance of debt contracts in the development of industrial economies and argued that large infrastructures like railways could have been hardly completed without recourse to such contracts. Debt contracts (whether loans or bonds) are typically not contingent on business performance, and this fixed nature was necessary to mobilize capital that would not have been attracted by equity contracts.

The reasons why money markets and payment systems must be information insensitive are somewhat different. In the case of debt, information insensitivity enables businesses to gain from the stability of the financing platform, being risk-averse investors not exposed to downside risk. In the case of money markets and payment systems, one faces problems of *trust*. At its core, the problem of money is a problem of trust that does not admit "intermediate" states. Trust must be unchallenged in order for the system to operate smoothly; even a little doubt can spread and amplify, and eventually lead to market freezes. Central banks are by now well aware of these potential chain reactions and stand on-the-ready to intervene. Strange as it seems, opacity has merits.[3]

This differentiation between stock and money markets is well established; still, it seems to conflict with standard views about transparency. Transparency is often considered a plus in all circumstances, and some argue that all financial markets should aim at maximizing transparency. Well, the aforementioned differentiation of financial markets shows that this is definitely not the case, at least as far as the stability of the market is at stake. A prominent case study concerns the summer of 2007, when

[3] Consider the celebrated statement by Mario Draghi of July 2012: "The ECB is ready to do whatever it takes to preserve the euro, and believe me, it will be enough." It has been pointed out that such a statement is as opaque as a statement can be, and this is perfectly in line with the principle of NQA.

a number of Money Market Mutual Funds (MMMFs) went under stress once rumors emerged about the properness of the LHS of their balance sheet, i.e. the quality of the assets held as collateral for the "shares" issued. The simple transition from a state of "no questions asked" (NQA) to a state of doubt triggered a run on a number of such funds that has resulted in the credit crunch of 2007, as premise of the catastrophe.

Since their takeoff in the 1980s, MMMFs have been considered *stabilizers* of the financial system, and the soundness of their method of liquidity transformation seemed to be out of question. In the summer of 2007 it has been the emerging information sensitivity of the asset side of their balance sheet that has shaken the industry, with analysts and columnists reporting the discovery of positions in collateralized debt obligations that were not expected to enter the balance sheet of a MMMF. Collateralized debt obligations are products of financial engineering (typically, synthetic securities representing tranches of pools of mortgages), and their market prices are hard to compare with fundamentals, and therefore raise questions. True, in recent years, the unexpected consequences of "marking to market" have been acknowledged as a pivotal financial instability at the roots of the great turmoil.

Well, the theory of money is currently undergoing a phase transition in which the principle of NQA unfolds its implications on the dynamics of liquidity and the role of *safe assets* and collateralization. It is for sure not a novelty to acknowledge that one wants NQA on the acceptability and redeemability of a money instrument. On the other hand, in the aftermath of the great financial crisis, genuine progresses in the rethinking of liquidity problems have taken place under the inspiration of the principle of NQA, in first instance concerning payment systems, the microstructure of bond and money markets, and global flows of collateral. In December 2019 Augustin Carstens (General Manager of the BIS) delivered a lecture on the future of money and the payment system at the University of Princeton; in the opening statement, Carstens admits that a few years before he could have not imagined delivering a lecture on such themes. Within this lecture, one single statement deserves great attention.

According to Carstens, the most effective way to improve the retail payment system is to build out the current account-based system to accommodate faster payments (in fact, velocity is one of the dimensions in which new tokens seem to outpace standard systems) and set a level playing field with room for both traditional banks and non-bank payment service providers. This is precisely our institutional perspective on the problem of embedding new digital instruments and functions into the global monetary system. After all, if a blockchain payment network is expected to operate in relative isolation from other circuits, economists may find little interest in exploring its potentials and shortcomings. Among the major shortcomings of the crypto eruption one may acknowledge the mechanisms involved in the crypto downfall of 2022, but the collateralization of *stablecoins* is perhaps the key character of the plot.

Stablecoins have been conceived so as to overcome the problems of price instability displayed by cryptocurrencies. The mechanism supposed to achieve the goal is collateralization: the value of a stablecoin is supposed to be backed by recognizable fundamentals, namely, those underlying the safe assets that back the value of the coin. Well, the problems of safe attests and collateralization project us at the core of the current rethinking of money.

2.2.2 Safe Assets and Collateralization

"For overall 'lubrication' of its functioning, the financial system requires collateral or money for intraday debits and credits. The cross-border financial markets traditionally use 'cash or cash equivalent' collateral (i.e., money or highly liquid fungible securities) in lieu of cash to settle accounts. Financial collateral does not have to be highly rated AAA/AA as long as the securities (which can be either debt or equity) are liquid, mark-to-market, and part of a legal cross-border master agreement, they can be used as 'cash equivalent.' In this way, collateral underpins a wide range of secured funding and hedging (primarily with OTC derivatives) transactions. Increasingly, collateral has a regulatory value as well as being cash-equivalent. Such financial collateral has not yet been quantified by regulators and is not (yet) part of official sector statistics, but is a key component of financial plumbing" (Singh, 2017).

Collateralization is one of the directions in which monetary economics is reassessing its grip on the concrete functioning of contemporary financial and money markets. Let us simply recall that *repo* (repurchase agreement) markets represent truly essential money markets in which heterogeneous entities (from commercial banks to hedge funds) manage their liquidity needs. A repurchase agreement is a secured short-term (possibly, overnight) loan, namely, an arrangement in which an entity buys cash in exchange for securities (the collateral) with well specified characteristics. At expiry, the borrower is expected to return the cash borrowed plus the repo rate, and thereby regain ownership of the pledged securities, possibly, different securities with the same characteristics. The *haircut* measures the difference between the market value of a security and its collateral value. Repo markets have displayed unexpected stresses in recent years, like the "squeeze" of the US repo market in September 2019—we refer the reader to Copeland et al. (2012) for a beautiful introduction to the sophistication of repo markets. The relevance of collateralization in the contemporary financial system is a good point of view on the recent reappraisal of the relevance of safe asset.

A key heritage of the financial crisis is the increased role of safe asset in the global financial system. Following the Federal Reserve, other central banks have decisively enlarged the size of their balance sheet in subsequent rounds of quantitative easing policies that have increased the supply of bank reserves of an order of magnitude or so. Bank reserves are a safe asset that banks employ in their liquidity management. Other intermediaries, as yet, have no access to the balance sheet of the central bank, and therefore safe assets like highly rated sovereign debt or corporate bonds have become the reference asset class of markets in the 2010s, and again in the 2020s.

The percentage of high-quality liquid assets (HQLAs) featuring in the balance sheet of large banks, in particular systemically important ones, has progressively increased since 2009; below is a figure for the US banking system. Recent banking regulations play a key role in this (fractional) increase. In this scenario, it is scarcely surprising to acknowledge economists from different research areas emphasizing a global safe asset shortage, and more generally a theoretical case for renewing the notion itself of a safe asset (Fig. 2.2).

Gorton (2017) provides a stimulating overview of the history of money as an history of safe assets. The Author defines a safe asset as one that can be traded without risk of adverse selection (no counterparty can have superior information about the "quality" of the asset) and represents a secure store of value. In a bold claim, the Author argues that much of human history is the search and the production of safe assets. This claim conveys the relevance of the theme in the current rethinking of monetary economics.

We want readers to appreciate that the safety of an asset (be it a jewel, a banknote, a security, a copyright, a hotel) is not a property of the asset in isolation, but a more complex property emerging from the ecology in which the asset is traded, and correlated with the collective

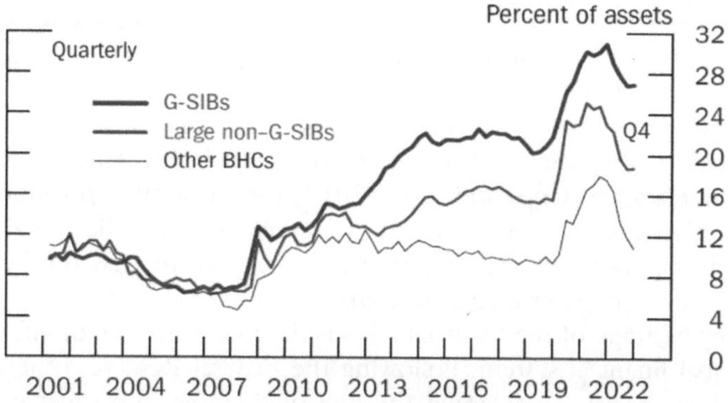

Fig. 2.2 The percentage of HQLAs in the balance sheet of Global Systemically Important Banks (G-SIBs), large non-G-SIBs and other Bank Holding Companies (BHCs). Reproduced from the Financial Stability Report, Board of Governors of the Federal Reserve System (May 2023)

phenomena therein. In fact, it is a truly challenging line of research to consider the safety of assets like US treasuries the result of *coordination* among investors/dealers (see for instance He et al., 2019). This game theoretic approach may represent a profound view on the generality of the monetary problem of coordination in which agents accept a means of payment in the expectation that others will accept it as well.

2.2.3 *The Inherent Hierarchy of Money*

A tradition in monetary thinking envisions "money" as a *two-sided balance sheet phenomenon* in which a debit-credit arrangement manifests itself as the counterparty relationship between a liability of the borrower and an asset of the lender. John Maynard Keynes and Hyman Minsky belong in this tradition (see Bell, 2001), that has to do with the historical debate between chartalists and metallists (see the Appendix to this chapter), as well as with the truly concrete network of financial institutions that play the role of market makers. The hierarchy of (account-based) money developed by Perry Mehrling (2013a) provides a clear picture of this conceptual construct, in which what counts as money and what counts as credit depends on one's position in the hierarchy.

The hierarchy of money enables one to sharpen intuitions about concrete phenomena that most people should be familiar with. When Adam deposits 1 dollar in his bank account, the balance sheet of the bank enlarges by the same amount on both sides, and Adam's bank account represents "bank money" that, typically, can be redeemed at par on demand. The liability of the bank is one side of this two-sided relationship, the other side being account-based money, namely, an asset owned by Adam either as an entry of the asset (LHS) side of the balance sheet of the legal entity "Adam," or as a legal claim that features in the unofficial book-keeping of the customer/household Adam.

Thus, large scale monetary phenomena, and financial flows in general, transmit via balance sheets. The theory of efficient markets, that for decades has dominated financial thinking, was somewhat indifferent to this basic fact. Well, in recent years, the relevance of the concrete microstructure of financial markets has been reappreciated on both theoretical and empirical grounds, in particular the concrete structure of bond markets for the liquidity of the securities traded. This market structure consists of the network of dealer balance sheets, and it is relevant to devise maps of this network within which researchers, professionals, and interested people in general, may sharpen their own intuitions about financial and monetary flows. Mehrling (2013a) provides one such map.

There is a hierarchy of monetary institutions that channel the various forms of money and securities in the financial system. The central banks stand on top of the architecture. In a truly simplified account, the asset side of the balance sheet of the central banks consists of government bonds, gold and other assets. The liability side consists of notes in circulation (physical cash), bank reserves and other liabilities (compare Fig. 1.2 for the US central bank). Thus, part of the liabilities of the central bank are *money*, and specifically, "base money" (the expressions monetary base and high-powered money are also used), the best money of the system. The central bank is the originator node of the architecture, which unfolds in the following scheme, in which boldface characters identify the items that participate in two-sided balance sheet relationships. Notes in circulation, despite being part of the base money aggregate, are not written in boldface since, at times, they may not be accounted for in a balance sheet. The stylization below does fit the mission of economists to simplify environments and processes—one can compare the plot elaborated by the BIS (2022, Graph 7) in which the monetary system is represented by a tree whose roots are given by the central bank.

Central Bank assets: government bonds, other securities, gold reserves, …
Central Bank liabilities: notes in circulation, **bank reserves**, other liabilities.

Bank assets: **bank reserves**, cash, securities, loans, tangible assets, hedging positions.
Bank liabilities: **short-term deposits**, term deposits, long-term debt, equity.

Dealer assets: **short-term deposits**, securities, derivatives, other claims.
Dealer liabilities: **short-term debt**, other liabilities, capital.

The "Dealers" that represent the progress in the hierarchy are the market makers whose balance sheets represent the concrete channels through which funds and securities flow in the system. As a concrete example, one can think of the theoretical "dealer" as a MMMF, that holds accounts at large banks as assets, and issues "shares" as short-term financing. These shares are meant to be somewhat close substitutes for demand deposits at commercial banks. In this sense, a dealer issues "money" with definite characteristics and that is accounted for in a definite monetary aggregate. Analogously, one can envision hedge funds, derivative dealers, asset managers, or whatever entity (possibly, a cryptoexchange), in place of the stylized "dealer" above.

Practitioners of monetary analysis will find it intuitive to envision how this hierarchy unfolds the monetary aggregates as one progresses downwards, what the velocities of these aggregates represent, and the several transmission channels of monetary policy.[4] The same practitioners may not be correspondingly acquainted with recent visions on the transmission of macroeconomic effects via balance sheets. The counterparty relationships represented in the hierarchy of money provide an intuitive picture for envisioning such transmissions. In particular, in times of stress, firms may be forced to reduce debt and shrink their balance sheets, and thereby reduce activities in ways that standard macroeconomics does not explicitly account for (see for instance Eggertsson and Krugman, 2012; Koo, 2015). The generality of the picture of the hierarchy of money can be further appreciated with respect to the vision of Hyman Minsky according

[4] The jargon of monetary policy features expressions like "interest rate channel," "asset price channel," or "balance sheet channel," that denote chains of transmission of the policies of the central bank to the financial sector or the real economy. These channels do interact.

to which every entity with a balance sheet can be considered a bank, at least as far as liquidity management is at stake.

In the hierarchy, the relative "prices" (or "exchange rates") of different monies can find a representation. Consider for instance the well established fact that people display a preference for a nominal anchor on demandable deposits, i.e. people want such deposits to be denominated and redeemable in the same units and size of the banknotes that they may withdraw at convenience. This is tantamount to saying that the relative price of deposits and base money must be 1, or *par*. Generalizing, the same par is *normatively* expected to hold as a nominal anchor bridging the different forms of monies that unfold along the hierarchy. On positive grounds, as is well known, this is not always the case, and "monies" are at times exchanged at a discount. A paradigmatic example of this phenomenon is given by the "free banking" era of the US, when a number of regional banks were allowed to issue their own bills with the same nominal unit "dollar," but such bills were exchanged at different discounts according to the location of trade.

Monetary economists may display heterogeneous attitudes concerning the relevance of the above stylized representation of financial markets. In our view, the picture represented by the hierarchy of account-based money is absolutely clear in representing the architecture along which flows of funds, liquidity and collateral are channeled in the everyday operation of the financial system. For instance, Mehrling (2013b) sheds light on the way foreign exchange (FX) markets encompass arrangements in which the balance sheet of private dealers and central banks operate in coordination.

Let us conclude the subsection with a cautionary note. Despite the properness of the picture represented by the hierarchy of money above, not everything is settled about the theoretical and empirical role of the entities therein. One may find it puzzling to acknowledge that a debate is still ongoing about what is a bank (see Sect. 6.4).

2.2.4 Bank Runs

In an interview at the Brookings Institution in 2014, Ben Bernanke, Fed Chair during the turmoil of 2007–2009, reviews the sequence of events and emphasizes the relevance of having a policy guide (a "playbook") in such dramatic times, in which every decision can be an irreversible pivot of events. Bernanke testifies that a major guide has been a revision of the classical Bagehot rule—lend freely, at a high rate, against good collateral in times of crisis—adapted to the properties of modern markets. Commitment to this rule is the Holy Grail of central banking.

A landmark analysis of lending of last resort and guarantees as mechanisms to prevent runs is an article by Douglas Diamond and Philip Dybvig[5] (1983) that tailors a dramatic stylization of what an economy produces and what a bank does. The model represents a paradigmatic example of the mission of economists of stylizing environments and interactions, and this is a good reason to devote a few lines to its elaboration. True, our point is to shed light on the basic degrees of freedom at play, and therefore on the sense in which the safety of an asset—recall, a bank deposit is an asset of the depositor and a liability of the bank—is not simply a property "localized" at the asset, but a more sophisticated problem of collective phenomena. In fact, preliminary insights on the essence of a bank run can be gleaned via an analogy with the prisoners dilemma.

As is well known, the prisoners dilemma displays a unique Nash equilibrium in dominant strategies in which opponents sacrifice a desirable outcome due to their inability to coordinate on an efficient strategy profile. Along similar lines, if deposits are not guaranteed, any depositor finds it rational to run on the bank under the fear that other depositors may fear that others may run, thereby threatening to bury the claims (the dollars) of the depositor under the ruins of a bank failure. In doing this, depositors sacrifice the going concern of the bank, that may even be perfectly healthy. This is one of the apparent paradoxes of economic dynamics that is in fact a perfectly rational outcome: rationality does not imply Pareto efficiency.

Thus, even beginners in game theory, with no specific background in monetary economics, can grasp the intuitive strategic dimension of bank runs (and runs to safety in general). These foundational insights represent a good starting point for a more comprehensive picture of the delicate liquidity service provided by banks, and the role of contingencies and asymmetric information (problems that do not impinge on the prisoners dilemma) in the way such delicacy manifests itself. Diamong and Dybvig (1983) provide one such model, in which the bank is perfectly healthy (albeit in a stylized sense). Noticeably, the model displays Nash equilibria

[5] The Authors have been awarded the 2022 Nobel prize in Economic Sciences.

in dominant strategies like the prisoners dilemma. Let us sketch the model as follows.

The model features three dates. At date 0 the economy can invest in production technology. On date 1 the project produces nothing if operated and breaks even if liquidated. At date 2, if operated, the technology produces a valuable output that remunerates appropriately the initial investment. Investors in the technology gain nothing in period 1 and may benefit from an artificial "transformation" of the project that may enable them to smooth consumption over periods. Well, a bank deposit contract can provide this service: in the stylization of the Authors, consumers finance the bank via demandable deposits (the relevant liabilities of the bank balance sheet) and become at the same time owners of the bank and of the project (the relevant asset of the bank balance sheet). In this sense, the bank transforms illiquid assets into liquid liabilities, at the cost of being subject to runs. If all depositors withdraw their funds at date 1, the bank is forced to liquidate assets at fire sale prices and goes bankrupt. At completion of the project (date 2) the bank is liquidated, and remaining depositors get a pro-quota share of the liquidation value.

Contingencies in the model reduce to the realization of a definite scenario: at date 1 each agent learns his "type," i.e. his preferences or needs for immediate consumption, and this pivots his choice of whether or not to withdraw funds from his deposit account. Type 1 depositors care only about consumption in date 1, whereas type 2 depositors care for consumption at both dates 1 and 2.

Incentives to withdraw are connected with the *sequential service* constraint, according to which the payoff from withdrawing depends on one's place in the line of requests. This is a crucial feature of the model game, and in fact of the literature in general, in that it shapes the way the interaction of depositors unfolds. The constraint provides an equation representing the choice problem of both types (patient and impatient) of depositors, for whom the value of deposits and the liquidation value of assets depends on the place in the line. Noticeably, this constraint has empirical soundness, and this theoretical and empirical relevance marks the place of this model in the history of monetary thinking. This completes the specification of the strategic problem.

The Authors begin to solve the model in the benchmark deterministic case in which the fraction of type 1 agents (those that develop liquidity needs) is common knowledge, and therefore a "normal" volume of withdrawals can be anticipated. In this case, suspension of convertibility, as contract clause, is shown to achieve the optimal allocation as Nash equilibrium in pure strategies. On the other hand, in the general case in which the fraction of type 1 agents is stochastic, the models display several equilibria, among which a bank run. The key point made by the Authors is that a credible guarantee on deposits, for instance in the guise of government insurance, enables the system to attain the efficient outcome as a pure strategy Nash equilibrium, and in particular, a dominant strategy equilibrium, i.e. one in which (like in the prisoners dilemma) each player has its own best strategy (not to run) that is unaffected by the choices of opponents. This way, deposit insurance solves an equilibrium selection problem, and in particular selects a state of NQA.

The model of Diamond and Dybvig shows that a deposit contract is in a position to outperform the allocation feasible via a market for contingent claims. However, our main interest is in the fact that deposit insurance (or, somewhat equivalently, the commitment of a credible lender of last resort) is a mechanism that prevents runs and selects efficient equilibria in which the bank can follow a desirable asset liquidation policy that can be separated from the cash-flow constraint generated by withdrawals. It matters for the public to trust the efficacy of the safety mechanism in place. It matters to have NQA.

2.2.5 *Trust*

It goes without saying that the above crude account of the monetary problem of the 2020s makes no justice of the current debate. It was our simple aim to fix a few ideas that readers may find hard, or time-consuming, to distill from research articles or websites. In particular, the above account enables us to sharpen the difference between the problem of trust that a PoW blockchain is meant to address and the problem of trust facing monetary institutions.

In the words of Nakamoto, Bitcoin is an electronic payment system based on cryptographic proof instead of trust, allowing two parties to transact directly without the need for a trusted third party. The Bitcoin design has been acknowledged as a brilliant combination of advances in computer science and game theory and has (thus far) succeeded in supporting the working of the platform somewhat reliably. We have seen in which (computer science) sense decentralization is meant to substitute trust in a central authority supposed to guarantee the properness and security of digital information transfer and record-keeping. The fast developing economics of information security is proving effective in mapping the incentives at play in such settings. In more established economic jargon, one speaks of adequacy and transparency in corporate accounting, a theme whose relevance has been amplified by a wave of corporate scandals at the turn of the millennium. Well, trust in a money instrument is another thing.

Trust in a form of money is not only trust that such money is accepted in its own circuit and that records of transactions and ownership distribution are reliable. One needs trust that such money is *safe* and redeemable in central bank money (the best money in place) on demand. One wants NQA on the possibility of exercising this option at will. Thus, liquidity needs are at the foundations of the monetary problem of trust: the model by Diamond and Dybvig (1983) is the landmark account of the basic forces at play, and the hierarchy of money depicts the way liquidity is channeled through the system of account-based money.

The monetary problem of trust is essentially forward looking: users expect the best money to raise no questions, namely, to be available, accepted, and issued by trustworthy and efficient institutions governing the stability of exchange rates and keeping inflation under control. On the contrary, the blockchain problem of circumventing trust in a central party is to a large extent backward looking, in that the acceptability of the token is taken for granted, and the properness of record-keeping and the immutability of the history of transactions is the crucial point. Correctness is at the essence of the computer science problem of trust, whereas the monetary problem of trust is a more nuanced problem of network effects that may onset even in a setting in which everybody is perfectly correct; that being the case, a central authority is required to manage these network effects efficiently. Recall, velocity of intervention is among the key factors in a financial panic.

In our view, deepening these insights on the above different problems of "trust" should rank high in the research agenda of the nascent economics of cryptocurrencies and digital money, if only for the relevant implication on regulation—in Chapter 6 we shall discuss the sense in which the regulation of stablecoins is a problem of NQA. The central bank digital currency that major central banks are currently engaged in designing may well employ some blockchain technology, but in its essence is an instrument meant to address monetary problems of NQA. Computer scientists as well may find it stimulating to deepen the differences between these ways of trust, that seem to find it hard to surface in the technical literature on blockchain, despite having some grip on the questions that cryptocurrencies should not raise.

We have been arguing in Sect. 1.1.1 that the monetary problem of trust can be neglected in a first approximation to the nature of the digital information transfer mechanism within a blockchain. Still, on grounds of regulation (a truly hot topic), one can ask whether more transparency and increasing information sensitivity should be expected to increase the stability and sustainability of a blockchain with a native token as means of exchange. The answer may not be obvious, and arguably require further refinement concerning *what* information for *what* recipients. The subtlety of this problem witnesses the relevance of a profound theoretical study of the crypto phenomenon in its manifold information-theoretic and economic implications.

Appendix: Chartalists and Metallists

Readers primarily interested in digital innovations and decentralized consensus may wonder whether a dated historical debate like the one between *chartalists* (or cartalists) and *metallists* may have anything to do with the potentialities of new digital money. This short Appendix addresses this question. We refer to Bell (2001) and Goodhart (1998) for an effective introduction to this debate, which shapes an enlightening standpoint on the innovation and evolution of monetary systems.

Goodhart (1998) addresses the project of the euro currency on the eve of the establishment of the monetary union not accompanied by a fiscal union. The theory of the "optimal currency area" has been a major inspiration for this design and has provided conceptual backing for the independence of the monetary and fiscal functions in the federal architecture of EU institutions. Goodhart challenges this position on both historical and theoretical grounds.

The theory of optimal currency areas can be considered a corollary of the metallist tradition, according to which a privately produced money instrument is meant to reduce transaction costs and thereby foster trade—and here one can already think of some analogy with stablecoins. This first axiom is accompanied by another axiom concerning the source of the "value" of a money instrument: metallists posit that one such instrument must have a *commodity value* like gold in order to develop the properties of means of exchange and store of value that one ascribes to a form of money—one can think of the value of stablecoins as generated by appropriate backing with safe assets.

With a different attitude, the chartalist tradition posits that it is the institutional backing of the instrument that triggers its acceptability as means of exchange, and its desirability as store of value. The "power" of the issuing authority is the foundation of the monetary status of a token, upon which the insignia of sovereignty certifies the institutional backing. In a sense, the metallist position is more sharply economically oriented in terms of cost-benefit analysis, whereas the chartalist position is a more nuanced economic-institutional perspective in which coordination is the logical cornerstone.

Well, according to Goodhart (1998) it matters to appreciate that throughout history a close link has repeatedly manifested itself between money creation and taxation. This connection is of particular use for the analysis of the recent transition of the international monetary system to a system of *fiat* currency; this line of reasoning pertains to the chartalist tradition. We do not embark on the sophisticated question of the weaknesses of the euro union, and simply notice that one should not consider the above considerations as historical curiosities. The inherent hybridity of FX markets (see Mehrling, 2013b), in which money is part market and part state, witnesses the concrete implications of acknowledging both sides (market and state) of the coin. In fact, the model of bank runs discussed by Diamond and Dybvig conveys a sharp sense in which the safety of bank money (bank deposits) is an institutional arrangement built on insurance and commitment of liquidity backstop, or lending of last resort.

Well, this brief historical digression may be useful in a thorough reflection on the reasons why institutional reviews on the future of money emphasize the need for a proper harmonization of the new forms of digital money with the extant account-based monetary system. Money is a social convention (Carstens, 2019; BoE, 2023) according to which people accept a means of exchange in the expectation that everyone else will do the same. Over the decades economists and central bankers have learned that it is institutional details that pivot the stability and efficiency of monetary arrangements. The problem of coordination is perhaps the conceptual cornerstone of the problem, in that coordination is inherently a matter of *centralized* governance and liquidity support—just think of the strategic relevance of central bank commitment to intervene in times of stress. The function of the central bank, that does not exhaust in the generation of base money, is a *public good*, and economists have long established the reasons why the private sector is not in a position to provide public goods. The nascent economics of cryptocurrencies and digital money provides new space for the theme to unfold.

References

Arnosti N., Weinberg S. M. (2022). Bitcoin: a natural oligopoly. Management Science 68 (7), 4755–4771.

Aumann R. J. (1982). Agreeing to disagree. Annals of Statistics 4 (6), 1236–1239.

Bell S. (2001). The role of the state and the hierarchy of money. Cambridge Journal of Economics 25, 149–163.

BIS (Bank for International Settlements, 2022). The future monetary system. Annual Economic Report.

Board of Governors of the Federal Reserve System (2023). Financial Stability Report. May.

BoE (Bank of England, 2023). The digital pound—speech by Jon Cunliff.

Capponi A., Ólafsson S., Alsabah H. (2021). Proof-of-work cryptocurrencies: does mining technology undermine decentralization? Management Science. Forthcoming.

Carstens A. (2019). The future of money and the payment system: what role for central banks? Princeton University Lecture.

Cong L. W., He Z., Li J. (2021). Decentralized mining in centralized pools. Review of Financial Studies 34, 1191–1235.

Copeland A., Duffie D., Martin A., McLaughlin S. (2012). The mechanics of the U.S. tri-party repo market. Federal Reserve Bank of New York Economic Policy Review, November.

Davidson M. (2023). State machine replication and consensus with Byzantine adversaries. NIST Internal Report 8460 ipd.

Diamond D., Dybvig P. H. (1983). Bank runs, deposit insurance, and liquidity. Journal of Political Economy 91 (3), 401–419.

Eggertsson G. B., Krugman P. (2012). Debt, develeveraging, and the liquidity trap: a Fisher-Minsky-Koo approach. Quarterly Journal of Economics 127 (3), 1469–1513.

Fischer M. J., Lynch N. A., Paterson M. S. (1985). Impossibility of distributed consensus with one faulty process. Journal of the Association for Computing Machinery 32 (2), 374–382.

Goodhart C. A. E. (1998). The two concepts of money: implications for the analysis of optimal currency areas. Europen Journal of Political Economy 14, 407–432.

Gorton G. (2017). The history and economics of safe assets. Annual Review of Economics 9, 547–586.
Haber S., Stornetta W. S. (1991). How to time-stamp a digital document. Journal of Cryptology 3, 99–111.
He Z., Krishnamurthy A., Milbradt K. (2019). A model of safe asset determination. American Economic Review 109 (4), 1230–1262.
Holmström B. (2015). Understanding the role of debt in the financial system. BIS Working Paper No 479.
Koo R. (2015). The Escape from Balance Sheet Recession and the QE Trap. Wiley.
Leshno J. D., Strack P. (2020). Bitcoin: an axiomatic approach and an impossibility theorem. American Economic Review: Insights 2 (3), 269–286.
Mehrling P. (2013a). The inherent hierarchy of money. Social Fairness and Economics. Economic essays in the spirit of Duncan Fowley. Routledge.
Mehrling P. (2013b). Essential hybridity: a money view of FX. Journal of Comparative Economics 41, 355–363.
Nakamoto S. (2008). Bitcoin: a peer-to-peer electronic cash system.
Narayanan A., Bonneau J., Felten E., Miller A., Goldfeder S. (2016). Bitcoin and Cryptocurrency Technologies. Princeton University Press.
Pagnotta E. S. (2022). Decentralized money: Bitcoin prices and blockchain security. Review of Financial Studies 35, 866–907.
Singh M. (2017). Collateral reuse and balance sheet space. IMF Working Paper 17/113.

CHAPTER 3

The Basic Mining Game

Abstract This chapter provides an exhaustive analytic treatment of the basic mining game. The landmark approach developed by Szidarovszky and Okuguchi is complemented with more recent discussions by Arnosti and Weinberg and Mantovi in order to build a twofold—both conceptual and analytical—perspective on the nature of the strategic equilibrium at stake. The former Authors establish an "absolute" approach in which the absolute quantities of resources deployed enter the conditions for equilibrium. The latter depict a "relative" approach in which shares of resources enter the relevant equations. Original plots provide intuitive clues for comparing such visions. The cost competitiveness of players is shown to drive the concentration of mining at equilibrium. The dual perspective enables one to deepen the implications of the aggregative property of the game: the global hashrate (the aggregate level of mining/hashing activity) emerges as the pivotal degree of freedom at play.

Keywords Bitcoin selection rule · Cost competitiveness · Best responses · Nash equilibrium. · Aggregative game

A. Schianchi and A. Mantovi, *The Economics of Cryptocurrencies and Digital Money*, Palgrave Studies in Financial Services Technology, https://doi.org/10.1007/978-3-031-44248-3_3

The incentives to participate in the ecology trigger the economic attractiveness of a blockchain, that, like a motor, continuously requires fuel to operate. According to Catalini and Gans (2020), in the mature phase of the network, this is the essential challenge that the blockchain protocol is meant to address, so as to avoid a tragedy of the commons in which agents are not in a position to coordinate on an efficient outcome. These considerations represent a good premise for the game theoretic inquiry of a permissionless PoW blockchain that we undertake in this chapter and the next.

In Chapter 1 we have introduced the conceptual relevance of the basic one-shot rent-seeking game and stated that it represents the foundation of the game theoretic inquiry on PoW. In this chapter we provide an exhaustive analytical discussion of the game, combining well-established results and recent ones within the in-and-out-of-equilibrium picture developed by Mantovi (2021). Original (to our knowledge) graphical representations convey sharp intuitions. A preliminary remark can help sharpen the significance of the following analytical results.

The game theoretic literature on PoW is essentially focused on the characterization of Nash equilibria. Still, the limits with which Nash equilibrium concepts can be used to interpret empirical evidence have been inquired for decades. For instance, the literature on experimental game theory reports that, at least under controlled conditions, real play does not necessarily converge to a Nash equilibrium. A number of game theorists are currently exploring solution concepts that can accommodate more general patterns than Nash equilibrium conditions. In such respects, our in-and-out-of-equilibrium description of mining points at enlarging the description of rational play that the extant literature is currently concerned with.

3.1 Mining Games

The game theory of mining builds on the properties of the PoW selection rule as a contest success function. An already established literature depicts mining competition as a Tullock contest, whose unique Nash equilibrium in pure strategies has been thoroughly characterized well before the introduction of Bitcoin. Nowadays such results are being reconsidered and refined in their positive and normative implications for blockchain phenomenology. Recent results by Mantovi (2021) constitute the core of our analysis, which envisions the aggregate scale of activity (the global hashrate) as the degree of freedom about which to cluster both analytical and qualitative arguments. Aggregative games have recently risen to the status of research subject of their own, as a way to sharpen the analysis of games in which players are perfect substitutes (in the sense of Cournot competition) or, more generally, display some degree of substitutability that can be characterized by an "aggregation" (or "aggregator") function in the response problem of each player (see Jensen, 2010; Cornes and Hartley, 2012). Aggregation yields in the first instance analytical simplification, and therefore augments the tractability of the problem and then the readability of results. This is one of the aspects that we shall emphasize in what follows.

The Bitcoin selection rule fixes the reward scheme for mining. Its implications have been subject to profound scrutiny over the last decade, and a number of researchers have stated that the Bitcoin protocol is not incentive-compatible, on account of the payoffs from starting attacks or forks. In our view, such weaknesses should not be ascribed to the essence of Nakamoto design (after all, our legislative systems are not shaken at the foundations by the empirical existence of crime), and rather traced along a hierarchy of model games, with a basic model at the foundations, in the spirit of Gintis (2009). In one such architecture, different economic models of the same problem are not substitutes and rather complements that enlighten each other's merits and limits.

As an example, a number of Authors have discussed potential modifications of the protocol that would "ameliorate" its incentive-compatibility, under the assumption that a single model (the "right" model) may fix the incentive-compatibility problem in terms of a strategic equilibrium (see Liu et al., 2019, and references therein). On the other hand, with a different spirit, Arnosti and Weinberg (2019) point out that a protocol can specify what miners are supposed to do, but not enforce such behavior. Such different perspectives have a place in a mechanism design approach: a desirable outcome may be attained as the equilibrium of different games with different strategic structures and punishment schemes.

As another example, it is well acknowledged that a few large mining pools may coalize and freeze any user's funds or erase past transactions. In our view, the incentives provided by such options should not be represented in a foundational model, and rather ascribed to options emerging at the boundaries of the ecology (an intuitive example of such boundaries concerns the repurposability of specific hardware). Mining rewards come at intervals as flows, whereas payoffs from attacks can be considered in the first instance a once-for-all gain, i.e. a stock: Budish (2018) in particular has emphasized the relevance of differentiating stocks from flows in the analysis of the incentive-compatibility of a protocol. On the other hand, entry options admit a foundational representation connected with cost competitiveness. This property has been interpreted as crucial for the concentration in Bitcoin mining, which according to Arnosti and Weinberg (2019) is a natural oligopoly. This property is at the core of our approach.

Risk-aversion has been recognized as a key motive for concentration, and then the emergence of mining pools, that has been interpreted as essentially providing risk sharing services. However, at a basic level of description, miners must be considered risk-neutral. The following section provides motivations for such a methodological first step.

3.2 An Axiomatic Approach

It is somewhat intuitive that the competition for the validation of a single block should deserve a special role in the strategic analysis of PoW. Such a game takes place repeatedly at somewhat regular intervals (approximately 10 minutes for Bitcoin), whose duration reflects a balance between the difficulty of the puzzle and the aggregate computational resources employed for solving it. This competition is the stage game of the (in principle, indefinitely) repeated game among miners. A theoretical investigation of PoW must therefore dig deep into the properties and the generality of this basic game.

It is well acknowledged that the permissionless nature of a blockchain is crucial for its efficiency (see for instance Saleh, 2021, and references therein), and one may argue that the foundational inquiry of PoW should start from the implications of this kind of free entry. In our view, though, it takes a basic analytic frame to fix the "coordinates" of the economic problem, and then elaborate on the implications of permission. The selection rule is considered to provide such a frame, as argued at length by Leshno and Strack (2020).

The Authors address the generality of PoW by an axiomatic approach to the properties of the Bitcoin selection rule, that, recall, reads

$$p_i(x) = \frac{x^i}{\sum_{j=1}^{n} x^j} \equiv \frac{x^i}{s(x)}, i = 1, \ldots, n \tag{3.1}$$

In words, the probability p_i with which miner i can be expected to be the first to solve the puzzle equals his fraction of total activity. The functional form of the rule reflects the way of the computational contest, namely, brute force. There is no intelligent way to solve the hashing puzzle (after all, this is one of the points of cryptography) and brute force computational exploration is pursued until the correct solution manifests itself by chance. In this sense, the adjective *trivial* has been applied to these puzzles (Saleh, 2021). Thus, the more (costly) computational resources employed, the sooner (or more likely) the solution manifests itself. It is worth noticing that in the literature the variables x^j have been interpreted both as instantaneously variable computational power (ongoing number of operations per unit time) and as computational capacity (peak performance) installed, depending on the phenomenon under consideration (see Sect. 4.2).

The algebraic simplicity of formula (3.1) is an effective representation of the cryptographic contest and establishes a truly explicit conceptual and analytical link between computer science and the game theory of PoW. Let us follow Leshno and Strack (2020) in the inquiry on the crucial strategic features of this selection rule.

The first property is the symmetry of participants in the contest. Miners, in a foundational representation, share the same strategy set, i.e. the range $(0, \infty)$ of potential levels of activity, and are symmetric (perfect substitutes) in the selection rule that fixes the probability of solving the puzzle as a function of the resources deployed (recall the emphasis on resources in the recent advances of the computer science of consensus, see Sect. 2.1.3). Such a symmetry assumes that miners employ hardware with the same efficiency, and is part of the egalitarian philosophy of decentralization, according to which miners should share the same opportunities. This symmetry is a clear instance of "justice", and, noticeably, is a property of the selection rule, but not of the overall game. Players are not symmetric in the costs they face, and this asymmetry gauges their competitive advantages. In a truly sharp sense, the game theory of PoW builds on the interplay between the symmetry of the selection rule and the asymmetry of cost functions, which manifests itself immediately in the first-order conditions for rational play that reflect basic intuitions about equalizing marginal revenues and costs. We shall build on such intuitions in the next section in the analysis of the analytical limits of best responses for small and large global (aggregate) scale of activity.

A second property satisfied by the Bitcoin selection rule is the absence of incentives to assume multiple fake identities as a means (Sybil attack) for improving chances of winning the contest. This property of the rule enables one to grasp how different properties can emerge at different levels of description. Sybil attacks have been repeatedly discussed over the last years as a significant strategy, and it is therefore relevant to recognize that they have no place in the foundational description we are targeting. Again, tolerance to Sybil is a focus of current research in computer science.

A third property is the absence of incentives to conglomerate in order to exploit alleged economies of scale, and amounts simply to the associative property of number addition. Leshno and Strack (2020) establish that the Bitcoin selection rule does satisfy the above three properties and that it is the only rule that satisfies them all for risk-neutral miners. In addition, the Authors establish the impossibility result that no rule can satisfy all these properties for risk-averse miners. Well, among other things, these results shed light on the benchmark role of risk-neutrality. The positive relevance of the implications of risk-aversion is out of question (and, after all, how can anyone care only about expected outcomes); still, the methodological relevance of expected utility theory is a well established theme that in the present context manifests itself via the above foundational properties. It is at the risk-neutral level of analysis that the Bitcoin selection rule manifests its generality. Risk-aversion can be properly accounted for in more refined settings, as will be seen.

We do not reproduce the proofs of these results, which would lengthen the chapter and relax the stimuli to engage directly in such a challenge. For our purposes, it is worth noticing that the above three axioms revolve around the scale invariance (homogeneity of degree 0) of the selection rule, namely, the fact that any scale transformation of individual activity levels leaves the rule invariant. In an intuitive example, doubling all activity levels leaves unaltered the probabilities of being the winner (but may alter payoffs).

Such a scale invariance specializes the general property that each player responds to the aggregate choice of opponents. Then, formally, each player can be considered to respond to the *overall* scale of activity, comprising his own level choice. *Aggregative games* are therefore our landscape, and additive aggregation is the analytical property at the foundations of our approach, in which the scale s of aggregate activity (the denominator of the selection rule) is the variable by means of which we shall explore the structure of the contest, namely, best responses and cost competitiveness.

3.3 Best Responses

We are dealing with a Tullock contest in which the above selection rule fixes the expected reward of miners as function of their shares of global activity (the expression "proportional rule" is at time used). Such activities come at a cost, and each miner i is characterized by its own cost function c_i. Following part of the literature, we assume the exogenously given reward as numeraire and write the expected profit for miner i as the dimensionless expression $p_i(x) - c_i(x^i)$. Notice that the expected reward is a function of all activity levels of players, represented by the vector of activities (strategy profile) x, whereas the cost function of miner i is a function exclusively of his own activity level x^i. In addition, notice that being the cost function dimensionless, marginal cost has the dimension of reciprocal activity level. This is a remark that, albeit straightforward, will be at the core of our analytical discussion.

Let us follow the literature in the approach to the equilibrium of the game, starting with the first order condition (FOC) for stationary expected profit

$$s^2 \frac{dc_i}{dx^i} = s - x^i \tag{3.2}$$

This condition is obtained by simple differentiation of profit with respect to the level of activity x, and then imposition of the condition of stationarity. Part of the readers may be scarcely attracted by this simple analytical expression and may miss the crucial point that the entire game theory of PoW rests on this condition, and in particular, our original results.

For $i = 1, \ldots, n$, formula (3.2) fixes the best responses $\mathrm{BR}^i(s)$ of players as functions of the aggregate scale of activity s, namely,

$$BR^i(s) = s - s^2 \frac{dc_i}{dx^i} \tag{3.3}$$

in conjunction with the participation constraint $dc_i/dx^i(0) < 1/s$ that triggers the threshold activity level below which miner i is worth mining.

It is insightful to consider the analytic form of best responses in the limit $s \to 0$. It is evident that the second term in the RHS of (3.3), in this limit, is negligible compared to the first. Therefore, in the limit $s \to 0$ the best response of each agent does not depend on costs, and approximates s. Thus, the aggregate best response of players is ns in this limit. It is a symmetric limit in which players share the same competitiveness. This simple analytical fact has relevant consequences. First, a situation of vanishing activity is not a Nash equilibrium: this property has long been established and deserves due emphasis in the strategic analysis of the attractiveness of a PoW environment.[1] It follows furthermore that in a pure strategy Nash equilibrium at least two players are active (a well-known property).

The symmetric game in which players face the same costs is a useful benchmark of analysis. First, the analytical characterization of equilibrium is simpler. In this case, one can aggregate identical FOCs, and write $x = \frac{n-1}{n^2} \frac{1}{\frac{dc}{dx}(x)}$ for the identical equilibrium strategy (activity level) x for all players. In particular, for linear homogeneous cost functions, one can write the well-known expression (being m_0 the common constant marginal cost)

$$xm_0 = \frac{n-1}{n^2} \tag{3.4}$$

The Nash equilibrium aggregate scale of activity s^* thus reads $(n-1)/(n\, m_0)$, and approaches $1/m_0$ for large n. This symmetric equilibrium is a benchmark result of the interplay between the scale invariance of the selection rule and the monotone increase of costs, with the explicit formula (3.4) accounting for the effects of scale transformations of m_0: definitely, the aggregate scale of activity of the symmetric Nash equilibrium is ***inversely proportional*** to m_0. This is a well-known fact that will provide inspiration for our considerations. Well known as well is the expression of the positive expected profit $1/n^2$ of each miner, which implies total profit $1/n$: as expected, in the limit of infinite players, the "market" approaches the perfectly competitive limit of vanishing profit

[1] We have defined strategic space with positive levels of activity, and therefore vanishing activity cannot be represented in our picture. One may enlarge the strategic space, but embedding a null state yields no additional conceptual elements to the discussion of the vanishing *limit* of activity. Szidarovszky and Okuguchi (1997), among others, demonstrate that a vanishing global activity cannot be an equilibrium.

(with a clear analogy with the competitive limit of Cournot oligopolies for a large number of players). This is an interesting point that deserves a few remarks.

Estimates of the Bitcoin carbon footprint often build on the assumption of a perfectly competitive environment, arguably, reflecting the permissionless property as a free entry condition. The symmetric game is compatible with such an assumption since players share the same cost function. However, for differentiated players, the perfectly competitive limit is not attained, since competitive advantages break the symmetry of perfect competition. In addition, it has been pointed out that such symmetry is crucial for decentralized consensus to emerge (see for instance Arnosti and Weinberg, 2019). These preliminary intuitions about symmetry breaking and perfect competition represent a natural introduction to the subsequent analytical development.

3.4 Uniqueness of Nash Equilibrium

Well before the introduction of Bitcoin, Szidarovszky and Okuguchi (1997) established a milestone in the characterization of the Nash equilibria of Tullock contests. The Authors developed an insightful analytical recipe for proving the existence and characterizing the uniqueness of the Nash equilibrium of the game. They assume players have different production functions entering the selection rule, and by a change of variable they reduce to our Bitcoin selection rule and convex cost functions. Our numeraire convention is adopted.

Our interest in the short but fundamental paper by Szidarovszky and Okuguchi (1997) is connected with the focus on the aggregate scale of activity s as the analytical pivot of the discussion of the aggregate best response of the system, i.e. the best scale of activity as response to an "initial" one. In other words, the Authors depict an analytical adjustment mechanism that resembles standard textbook descriptions of how a pair of Cournot duopolists may alternate in best responding one to another and thereby converge on the unique equilibrium of the system. Our game is a simultaneous game in which, therefore, players do not actually respond to the choice of opponents. Still, formally, the calculus of best responses and adjustments sheds light on the strategic structure of the problem, much like the reaction functions of Cournot duopolists are insightful elements in the discussion of such market structure.

The Authors define the function Υ as the sum of best responses to the scale s minus s itself, so that, by definition, $\Upsilon = 0$ is a condition of Nash equilibrium. They demonstrate that the function Υ is monotonically decreasing in a neighborhood of its unique vanishing point and that no other scale s can correspond to a Nash equilibrium. The Authors thereby reestablish the uniqueness of the Nash equilibrium in an analytical setting that the subsequent literature has acknowledged as a landmark approach.

We refer to the original article for the analytical details. For our purposes, it matters to notice that Υ embodies an absolute level of activity that, however, can be factorized as the product of the scale s and a dimensionless function, as represented in formula (3.5) below. This property is far from obvious and paves the way to the subsequent considerations. In fact, an explicit expression of Υ can be attained upon considering the analytical form (3.3) of best responses: one can write

$$Y(s) = (n-1)s - s^2 \sum_{k=1}^{K} \frac{dc}{dx^k} = s\left(-1 + \sum_{k=1}^{K} 1 - s\frac{dc}{dx^k}\right) \tag{3.5}$$

where the sum extends over active miners (recall, for inactive miners the participation constraint is not satisfied). This expression, which does not feature in the original article by Szidarovszky and Okuguchi (1997), will be crucial for our approach. The noticeable analytic fact represented in the formula is factorization. One can factor out the scale s and write Υ in the form sF, being F a dimensionless function that, by definition, accounts for relative (in the sense of fractional) best responses. This analytical fact has relevant conceptual implications that we shall develop in the subsequent sections, culminating in an identity that fixes the analytical cornerstone of our discussion. For the moment it matters to consolidate intuitions about the evolution from small to large scale of best responses.

In the limit of small s all players are identically competitive. For $s \to 0$ players face vanishingly small costs, and, being the aggregate best response ns, Υ approximates $(n-1)s$. Then, as s increases, differential cost competitiveness unfolds, and the slope of Υ at some point turns negative, since the function must at some further scale account for the unique Nash equilibrium, that is attained for $\Upsilon = 0$. Then, in the limit of large s, costs exceed the expected reward and no player is worth mining. This is a tale from symmetry to asymmetry that we shall deepen in graphical terms in Sect. 3.6, displaying the development of competitive advantages with the scale. One may call such advantages 'economies of scale', with a point of view that balances expected reward and costs, and that differs from the (non existing) benefits of conglomeration in the selection rule. The following section moves in such a direction.

3.5 Cost Competitiveness and Entry Thresholds

In a recent article, Arnosti and Weinberg (2019) apply the Tullock analytical setup to the analysis of Bitcoin mining. The same game of the previous sections is considered, but under the assumption that the n potentially active miners face linear homogeneous cost functions, therefore uniquely characterized by the marginal cost parameter m_i. The analytical tractability that follows from this assumption provides ample justification for this modeling choice. The numbers m_i can be ordered from lower to larger, and one obtains an ordering of players in terms of increasing (or not decreasing) marginal cost, and therefore decreasing competitiveness.

One can define an index of the competitiveness of each player as

$$\max 1 - \frac{m_i}{m}, 0 \tag{3.6}$$

in terms of the variable $m \in (0, \infty)$ as benchmark of cost competitiveness. Each value of m partitions miners into those with a marginal cost lower than m (that we may call the *fit*) and the rest. The index (3.6) is a dimensionless, continuous, and piecewise continuously differentiable function of m. It approaches 1 in the limit $m \to \infty$ (in which every marginal cost is fit), and monotonically decreases for decreasing m. The index vanishes for $m \in (0, m_i)$. The index, being dimensionless and ranging in the interval [0, 1), may admit an interpretation of a fraction of a total. It will turn out to be so.

Arnosti and Weinberg (2019) then define the function X as the sum over players of the above index:

$$X(m) \equiv \sum_{k=1}^{n} \max\left(1 - \frac{m_k}{m}, 0\right) \tag{3.7}$$

The function X embodies an aggregate measure of the cost competitiveness of players. The monotonicity of the index above implies the monotonicity of X. The function X is meant to play a role analogous to that of the function Υ of the previous section, namely, to characterize the unique Nash equilibrium of the game.

To begin with, by the monotone character of X, there exists a unique m^* such that $X(m^*) = 1$. Such a value is larger than m_2, since $X(m_2) < 1$. The Authors then demonstrate the fundamental result: the condition $X = 1$ identifies the unique Nash equilibrium of the game, at which the levels of activity read

$$x^i = \frac{1}{m^*} \max\left(1 - \frac{m_i}{m^*}, 0\right) \tag{3.8}$$

One thereby obtains further insight into the index (3.6) as proportional to the equilibrium levels of activity, an instance that we shall deepen in what follows.

Thus, the value m^* can be considered a competitiveness entry threshold, if one assumes that the unique Nash equilibrium is the "reality" that the model identifies as possible. The key point of Arnosti and Weinberg (2019) is that the asymmetry of marginal costs manifests itself in the concentration of mining. According to the Authors, empirical evidence about concentration must not be interpreted as a temporary aberration, since Bitcoin is a natural oligopoly: even apparently small asymmetries in marginal costs result in a significant increase in concentration. This is a crucial point: departure from cost symmetry generates instability, so the larger the asymmetry, the more the concentration. This is an exogenous picture of differentiated competitiveness that we are going to complement with a picture of endogenously emerging differentiation with the increase of the aggregate scale of activity s. Let us start with graphical representations.

Consider the example of four potentially active miners with marginal costs ¼, ½, ¾, 1 in some units (recall, in our convention, the marginal cost has a dimension of reciprocal activity level). Figures 3.1. and 3.2 plot the function X for the example, for different ranges of the independent variable m, thereby enlightening different details.

The first plot provides a global picture, with the asymptotic limit 4 on the right already in sight for $m = 10$. The monotone increase is represented clearly, but further details may not be that clear. The second plot enables one to grasp more easily the details of jumps in the slope at the points of entry of miners. The concavity of each trait manifests the concavity of the index (3.6). The slope of the function increases with a new entry, as follows from the additive form of X.

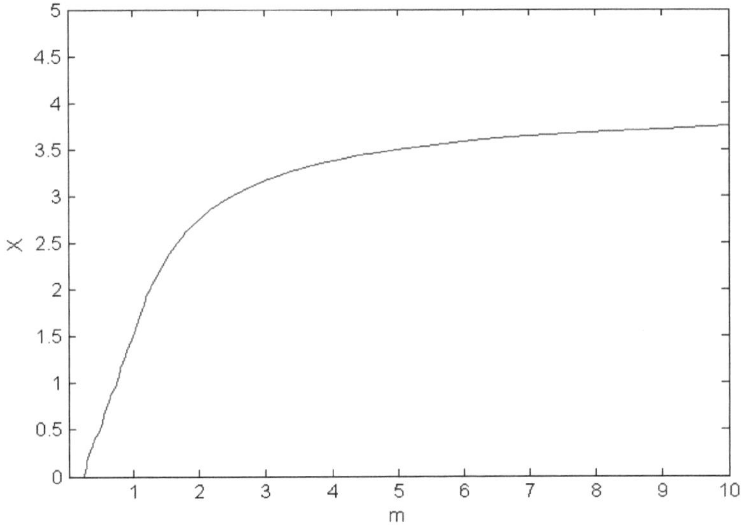

Fig. 3.1 Plot of the function $X(m)$ for the example, in the range $(0, 10)$. The large m asymptotic limit is clearly in sight

On the other hand, it is not easy to convey graphical insights about the condition $X = 1$ as characterizing the Nash equilibrium of the model. We shall gain such intuition in the subsequent section that fixes our key results.

3.6 The Connection Between X and Y

The extant literature seems to have discussed the functions X and Υ essentially as instrumental to the analytical characterization of the unique equilibrium of the system. In this section, we enlarge the perspective to out-of-equilibrium patterns. Mantovi (2021) uncovers a simple algebraic identity between the two functions that cross-fertilizes results already established and further provides a unifying framework that can accommodate a global strategic picture.

A change of variable is the key step. A number of elements in the previous sections lead us to this step. First, in units in which the fixed block reward is the numeraire, the marginal cost has the dimension of reciprocal activity level, i.e. the same dimension as $1/s$. Second, the

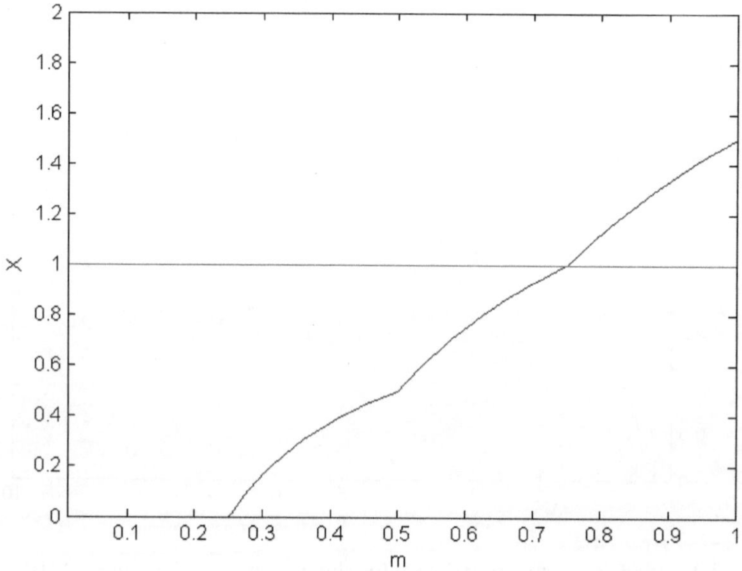

Fig. 3.2 Plot of the same function $X(m)$ in the range $(0, 1)$

symmetric example with constant marginal costs features a reciprocal relationship between such marginal cost and the equilibrium scale. Third, recall our description of best responses with the expansion of scale as a tale from symmetry and identical competitiveness in the small-scale limit, to asymmetry and differentiated competitiveness as s increases, and then with vanishing best responses above a definite threshold. Compare such a description with that of increasing m, in which one starts with the player(s) with lower minimal marginal cost as the unique competitive one(s), and subsequently adds competitive players for increasing m, up to the limit of large m in which all players are equally competitive. Such stories display a reciprocal character, in the sense that the small (large) s limit compares to the large (small) m limit.

Overall, a number of insights invite us to explore the consequences of the change in variable

$$m = \frac{1}{s} \tag{3.9}$$

in the function X. This kind of analytical exploration is at times useful to deepen intuitions about a model. In the present case, the change of variable allows for an explicit comparison of X and Υ as functions of the same variable s. We can write X as

$$X(s) \equiv \sum_{k=1}^{n} \max\left(1 - s\frac{\partial c_k}{\partial x^k}, 0\right) \tag{3.10}$$

allowing for the possibility of variable marginal cost, as in the setting discussed by Szidarovszky and Okuguchi.

Let us plot the function $X(s)$ for the above example of four potentially active miners with marginal costs ¼, ½, ¾, 1. Being $X(m)$ monotonically increasing, after the change of variable $s = 1/m$ we expect the function $X(s)$ to be monotonically decreasing. This monotone character is represented in Fig. 3.3, with a number of further details that justify the introduction of graphical analysis.

The same story represented in the previous figures is guest. With respect to the variable s, maximal competitiveness is attained the limit

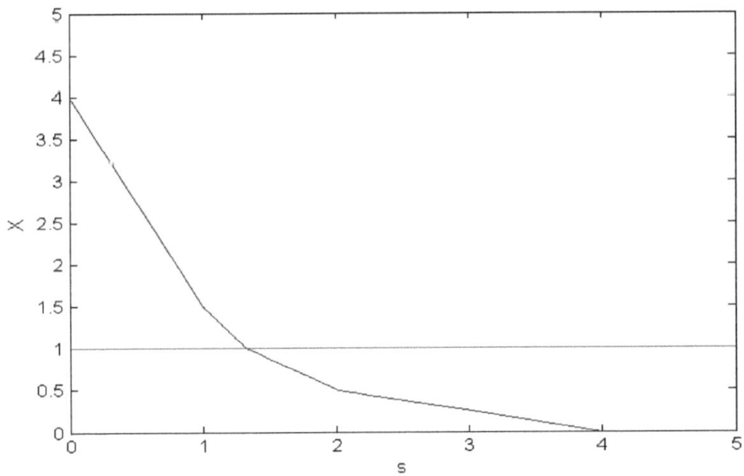

Fig. 3.3 Plot of the function $X(s)$ for the example. Notice the discontinuities in the slope of the piecewise linear function at the points of exit, and the Nash equilibrium at the reciprocal $4/3$ of $m^* = 0.75$. The function vanishes identically beyond the exit threshold $s = 4$

$s \to 0$, in which miners face no costs and are therefore identical. The monotone decrease of function X is a transparent representation of the decrease of aggregate competitiveness for increasing s. The function $X(s)$ is continuous and piecewise linear; piecewise linearity follows from the linearity of the cost functions of players. We are not aware of similar plots in the literature.

This story compares to the tale of scale expansion previously discussed in terms of the function Υ. It is natural to argue about explicit analytical links between the two representations. A key analytical fact is the factorization of the aggregate scale of activity s in the expression (3.5), which can be written $\Upsilon = sF$. This property suggests that the dimensionless function F may be connected with function X. This is indeed the case. In fact, the identity

$$Y(s) = s(X(s) - 1) \qquad (3.11)$$

holds. The analytical proof of such identity amounts to a detailed comparison of formulas (3.5) and (3.10). Such simplicity should not lead one to underestimate the relevance of the result (and, recall, simplicity is a plus for economic models). In the first instance, such an identity sheds new light on the Nash equilibrium condition $X = 1$. Write the identity as $\Upsilon + s = sX$, i.e. as the identity between the aggregate best response $\Upsilon + s$ of miners and the product sX. Well, by definition, at the Nash equilibrium, one has $\Upsilon = 0$, and the identity reduces to $s = sX$.

The simplicity of the algebra is a plus from an economic standpoint, in which sharp insights must be communicated neatly. One such insight goes that the monotone function X ranges between zero and the number of potentially active miners and does coincide with the ratio of the aggregate best response to s and s itself. At the Nash equilibrium, by definition, such scales do coincide, and the ratio is 1. Out of equilibrium such a ratio is not unitary, but however gauges the relative (fractional) aggregate best response: if the ratio exceeds 1, players are better off augmenting the scale of activity, i.e. aggregate best response exceeds s. The opposite for X lower than 1. These considerations are clearly represented in Fig. 3.3 and witness the profound significance of the change of variable $m = 1/s$ that is at the core of our approach. At the same time, the aggregative nature of the game enables one to grasp the cleverness of the Nakamoto design from an analytical standpoint.

The identity helps us to build the plot of the function Υ starting from the plot of X. Figure 3.4 represents a number of properties of best responses that we are by now accustomed to. The function Υ is continuous and piecewise continuously differentiable in $(0, \propto)$. In the limit $s \to 0$ the Taylor approximation $(n - 1)s = 3s$ of Υ holds: all players are active, and share the same approximate best response s in this limit. For increasing s, Υ increases with diminishing speed (slope), and attains a maximum when the aggregate best response to s exceeds s of the largest amount—this is a property to which the literature does not seem to pay great attention, perhaps since it is attained out of equilibrium. The function decreases from there on and displays a jump in the slope at the scale of exit of the less competitive miner.

Υ vanishes (by definition) at the unique Nash equilibrium of the game, at which Υ displays also (and this is not by definition) a jump in the slope corresponding to the next miner exit. Continuous decreasing and two more jumps lead to the threshold $s = 4$ at which no miner is worth

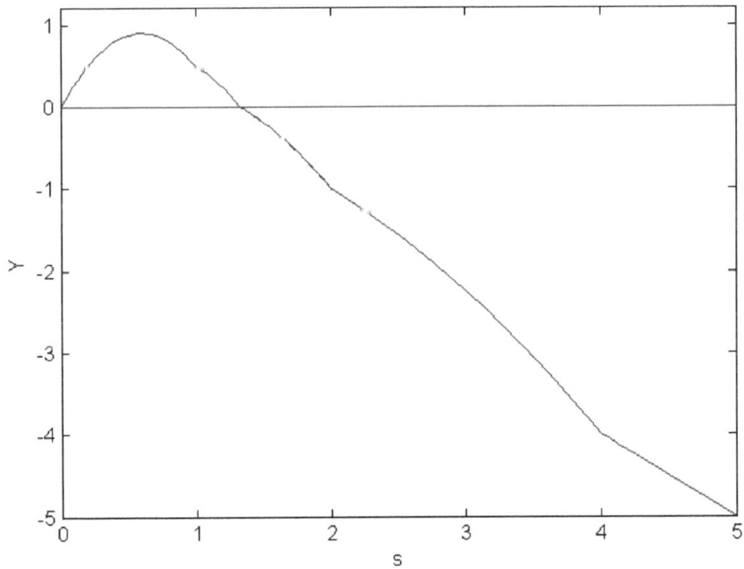

Fig. 3.4 Plot of the function $\Upsilon(s)$ for the example. Notice the discontinuities in the slope of the piecewise quadratic function at the points of exit

mining, since all best responses vanish identically from there on, and therefore $\Upsilon = -s$.

Among the merits of these insights is a sharp intuition about the Nash equilibrium condition $X = 1$. The condition has long been discussed in analytical terms, in essence, showing that it is equivalent to the FOC for expected profit stationarity (see for instance Arnosti and Weinberg, 2019). Such an approach is perfectly correct but does not convey a vision on the pattern of best responses. This can be achieved via the identity (3.11). The condition $\Upsilon = 0$ is *by definition* a Nash equilibrium condition: the simple proof that it is equivalent to the condition $X = 1$ cross-fertilizes both analytical instruments.

Recall, differential calculus places significant emphasis on the relevance of plots for building analytical intuition of the phenomenon that a function is meant to picture. And, after all, economic intuition does not build simply on equations, witness the ample use of plots in introductory textbooks. Well, the relevance of aggregation is represented in our plots, in particular linear aggregation, in which strategies are numbers that can be simply added as in a Cournot oligopoly. The scale s of activity is the aggregator.

These considerations enlighten the conceptual reach of our analytical discussion. The best responses of the basic game are the "strategic forces" that push toward the unique equilibrium of the contest: we have succeeded in connecting them transparently with the individual and aggregate indices of cost competitiveness. From an economic standpoint, the sharpness of such intuitions is a major plus of our approach. The following section reviews the main implications of our discussion.

3.7 Highlights

The Proof-of-Work competition among miners is designed by the Bitcoin selection rule as a Tullock contest. It has been known for decades that such a game admits a unique Nash equilibrium in pure strategies, a property that makes it particularly interesting on grounds of mechanism design. The recent phenomenology of cryptocurrencies has stimulated reconsiderations of such a property that may enlighten the general traits of the competition among miners, beyond the strict characterization of the sole Nash equilibrium. For instance, it has been repeatedly reported by specialized media that miners typically operate at full capacity, an occurrence that is not straightforward to interpret as a strategic equilibrium, and that we shall comment on in what follows. Furthermore, the permissionless Bitcoin arena is at times assumed to be perfectly competitive in estimates of its carbon footprint, and it is therefore the contest game itself that is called into question as a sound lens to observe phenomena. This is the sense of our methodological approach: to use models as building blocks of lines of reasoning, not for predicting outcomes. For instance, recall, the equilibrium of the symmetric basic game approaches the perfectly competitive limit for large numbers of miners and therefore marks a point in favor of the usefulness of our (Tullock) model. The saying goes that all models are wrong, but some can be useful. The literature has already acknowledged the usefulness of the basic game; it is our aim to deepen the traits of such usefulness.

Our approach to the problem has developed along the lines of Mantovi (2021). We have succeeded in fixing a simple algebraic relationship between the functions X and Υ, and therefore a transparent connection between the analytical form of best responses and the distribution of competitiveness among players. Let us sketch the key properties of mining that emerge from our discussion.

First, the identity $\Upsilon = s(X-1)$ connects absolute and relative levels of activity. Best responses have the dimension of activity level, and the identity establishes that the aggregate (absolute) best response $\Upsilon + s$ to the scale s does coincide with the product of s itself with the aggregate index X of cost competitiveness, which therefore manifests itself as the aggregate fractional (relative) best response. Such a transparent connection does not seem to feature in extant literature. In fact, the functions X and Υ have been considered functions of different variables, and therefore inherently not suited for a connection like this. The profound significance of the change of variable $m = 1/s$ in function X unfolds in such a connection, as well as in the following points.

Second, the global in-and-out-of-equilibrium perspective. The game theory of PoW and blockchain phenomena has been thus far developed essentially as a problem of Nash equilibrium. However, there is much more to game theory than the characterization of Nash equilibria. Consider for instance the relevance of strategic dominance and iterated elimination of dominated strategies, which are truly instructive exercises in shedding light on the complete strategic problem. Not to talk about the fact that games with multiple Nash equilibria call for equilibrium selection devices to tailor arguments about the reasonability of different equilibria (recall the incredible threats of entry deterrence discussed even in basic textbooks of industrial economics). Among the interesting implications of our in-and-out-of-equilibrium picture is an intuitive graphical representation of entry thresholds as explicit manifestations of the effects of permissionless entry.

Third, Arnosti and Weinberg (2019) advocate a comparative analysis of the Nash equilibria of the basic game as manifesting the strategic essence of concentration. It turns out that differentials in cost competitiveness provide a clear equilibrium justification for the increase of mining concentration in the hands of the more competitive. It is instructive to compare such a scenario for different games with our discussion of the development of within-game (endogenous) differentiated competitiveness, that is, the way cost competitiveness evolves and differentiates among players with the increase of the aggregate scale of operation. In 2021 a significant fraction of Bitcoin miners exited the market, and the incentives for new entrants with lower cost competitiveness have been discussed by specialized media. Arguably, our within-game picture and the discussion by Arnosti and Weinberg can be considered complements in shedding light on such empirical facts.

These points shape the logic with which in the next chapter we shall review a number of models of the Bitcoin environment. It is our aim to introduce the reader to the emerging specialized literature and to discuss the way the structure (the best responses) of the basic game can underlie and shape the structure of more articulated games. Our methodological challenge is to reverberate the strategic analysis of the basic model at higher levels of complexity (in the spirit of Gintis, 2009), in which miners interact with users, sellers of hardware, pool managers, etc.

References

Arnosti N., Weinberg S. M. (2019). Bitcoin: a natural oligopoly. Proceedings of the 10th Innovations in Theoretical Computer Science (ITCS).

Budish E. (2018). The economic limits of Bitcoin and the blockchain. NBER Working Paper 24717.

Catalini C., Gans J. S. (2020), Some simple economics of the blockchain. Communications of the ACM 63 (7), 80–90.

Cornes R., Hartley R. (2012). Fully aggregative games. Economics Letters 116, 631–633.

Gintis H. (2009). The Bounds of Reason. Princeton University Press.

Jensen M. K. (2010). Aggregative games and best-reply potentials. Economic Theory 43, 45–66.

Leshno J. D., Strack P. (2020). Bitcoin: an axiomatic approach and an impossibility theorem. American Economic Review: Insights 2 (3), 269–286.

Liu Z., Luong N. C., Wang W., Niyato D., Wang P., Liang Y. C. Kim D. I. (2019). A survey of blockchain: a game theoretical perspective. IEEE Access 7, 47615–47643.

Mantovi A. (2021). Bitcoin selection rule and foundational game theoretic representation of mining competition. Working Paper. Dipartimento di Scienze Economiche e Aziendali. Parma, Italy.

Saleh F. (2021). Blockchain without waste: Proof-of-Stake. Review of Financial Studies 34, 1156–1190.

Szidarovszky F., Okuguchi K. (1997). On the existence and uniqueness of pure Nash equilibrium in rent-seeking games. Games and Economic Behavior 18 (1), 135–140.

[illegible]

Martin, A. (20[illegible]) [illegible]

[illegible]

[illegible]

CHAPTER 4

Higher Level Models

Abstract This chapter brings to completion our game theoretic analysis. We introduce the "instrumental" approach to game theory advocated by Larry Samuelson as the methodological stance that shapes our discussion. We do not aim at an exhaustive review of the extant literature but rather at a selective review of relevant models of mining competition concerning the vertical structure of the industry, in which the game form features two stages, one of which coincides with (or closely resembles) the basic game discussed in the previous chapter. The exhaustive analytical treatment of the previous chapter is not replicated for evident reasons of limited space. We consider risk-neutral miners engaged in acquiring specialized hardware. Then, we consider risk averse miners and argue that mining pools emerge for risk-sharing purposes. The degrees of freedom at play and the resulting concentration of mining differentiate from those depicted by Arnosti and Weinberg for stylized miners. The interaction of miners and users is further addressed. Backward induction is given a thorough discussion.

Keywords Instrumental Game Theory · Specialized hardware · Mining pools · Backward induction

A. Schianchi and A. Mantovi, *The Economics of Cryptocurrencies and Digital Money*, Palgrave Studies in Financial Services Technology,
https://doi.org/10.1007/978-3-031-44248-3_4

This chapter elaborates on the results of the previous one in the discussion of more articulated models of a PoW ecosystem, with Bitcoin as a natural representative. We shall follow the literature in looking at mining as an *industry*, thereby inheriting basic intuitions from industrial economics. We have already pointed out profound analogies between the competition of miners and Cournot oligopolies; in this chapter, we enlarge the picture to sequential games, different types of players, and explicit equilibrium selection procedures. We are not in search of the "right" model of a PoW ecology, that is impossible to write down. Our aim is to pin down basic analytic methods for enabling emergent phenomena to manifest themselves as equilibria of some game.

In this effort, a key step is to embed a game into a larger sequential game as one of the stages. This approach has been long adopted in industrial economics, typically in a two-stage setting. In the second stage of the game, part of the players responds to the actions of the first movers. Backward induction is then a natural guide to the identification of rational play; one can thereby represent first-mover advantages as in Stackelberg duopoly. No wonder, the nascent literature on PoW has already explored this type of model, some of which will be part of our review. We shall envision such models as instances of a hierarchical complexity of problems, in the sense of Gintis (2009), and briefly digress on the subtleties raised by backward induction reasoning. Our methodological approach is meant to enlighten the potential of game theoretic models of rationalizing the emergence of relevant phenomena, but also to place due emphasis on the insights that one gains concerning market power, economies of scale and scope, vertical integration, and market evolution.

Once again, a metaphor seems to enlighten the way. There is no comprehensive analytical model of the physiology (as equilibrium, in some sense) of a human body, and we must content ourselves with qualitative descriptions of general regularities and healthy conducts. Furthermore, such physiology does not partition into equilibria of single systems (cardiovascular, respiratory, etc.), and concerns also the interactions between systems. Somehow analogously, there is no comprehensive model game of a PoW environment, and one is forced to elaborate qualitative pictures of the equilibria of the different strategic interactions at play. This is the point of this chapter: the exhaustiveness of the analytical treatment of the basic game is not replicated in what follows, and we shall rather concentrate on the emergence of somewhat general economic insights, concerning, for instance, the ability of large miners to force users into competition overs fees, the existence of strategic limits to Bitcoin scaling, the interaction between risk sharing and competition, and general forces that promote or counter decentralization (that one can perhaps discuss as *market failures*).

Our review is evidently constrained in scale and scope. The limited size of the chapter constrains the number of models that we can discuss, and our methodological stance triggers the aspects upon which to concentrate, in primis, linear aggregativity as DNA of PoW, that is to say, looking at the global hashrate as the *pivotal* degree of freedom at play.

4.1 Instrumental Game Theory

In the previous chapter, we have been discussing the analytical structure of the basic mining game and added a few preliminary remarks on the subtleties involved in the application of the model to specific contexts. There are general problems that arise in applied game theory, and there are more specific questions concerning PoW, that make the interpretation of equilibrium conditions not straightforward.

It is well known that the equations entering economic models do not share the "hard science" status of the equations of physics or chemistry. Among the main reasons is the fact that economic models are typically stylizations of empirical regularities emerging from complex environments. Well, competitions among miners have recently emerged in a number of PoW blockchains as empirical regularities, i.e. phenomena recognizable enough to admit empirical inquiry. Notice that not all phenomena display comparable recognizability: for example, off-chain coordination mechanisms among blockchain stakeholders do not seem (as yet) to admit systematic analysis.

Miners are attracted to the PoW arena by profit opportunities. The exact properties of this attraction are the essential target of the basic mining game. More articulated interactions, though, play a decisive role in such environments, like the interactions between miners on the one hand, and, on the other hand, users, hardware manufacturers, and mining pools. These interactions are more complex than those represented in the basic mining game, and one does not want to represent them in full detail. Simplicity is a virtue of economic models, not a vice. In such respects, Larry Samuelson (2016) provides an effective account of some of the wisdom that game theorists have developed over the decades.

The Author challenges the classical view that a game form is supposed to represent a complete specification of the strategic problem under consideration and that the tractability of the model should not be considered pivotal for the usefulness of the model itself. Well, the expression "instrumental game theory" is used to denote a more sophisticated vision of the task of game theorists. An explicit quote is worth it. "Classical game theory views the specification of the model as straightforward and focuses on what to do once one has the model. Under instrumental game theory, the specification of the model takes center stage. This specification requires an understanding of the application, setting, and history of the game, all of which should inform the specification not only of the game but also of the choice of equilibrium concept and equilibrium" (ivi, p. 120).

In other words, classical game theory adopts a deductive approach, in which the specification of the model is not in dispute, and the (essentially mathematical) problem is to identify the endogenous properties of the model, that are assumed to reflect properly the properties of the targeted economic reality. Instrumental game theory is more nuanced in acknowledging the complexity of reality, and therefore that deductive and inductive reasoning can be hard to disentangle in the complete flowchart of construction, solution, and interpretation of a model. In fact, among economists, there is talk about the *art* of economic modeling, in which simplicity and transparency are functional (instrumental) to the usefulness of the model. Unsurprisingly, one may envision a close connection with the interest growing among macroeconomists for small and modular models, which can be employed as building blocks of more articulated models. The basic mining game is the fundamental building block of our vision of blockchain models, in particular concerning payoff structures.

Payoffs are part of the definition of a game. In principle, payoffs are exogenously given. In practice, however, a game that represents a somewhat realistic competition may entail nuances in the definition of payoffs as part of the "art" of model building. The basic mining game has cardinal payoffs that are sharply defined just because it is elementary. More elaborate models encompass payoffs that reflect stylizations about the relevant incentives at play. This unavoidable logical circularity (an entanglement between deductive and inductive reasoning) can be considered part of the instrumental point of view. In this chapter, we assume this instrumental point of view for looking at the model games we review.

4.2 Vertical Integration: Sale and Operation of Specialized Hardware

It has been stated that the factual occurrence of concentration in Bitcoin mining is an *unintended* consequence of the incentives designed by the protocol and a serious concern for the Bitcoin community. Such an outcome seems to undermine the philosophy of decentralization at its foundations, and the fact that the outcome was unintended signals the complexity of the phenomena emerging in a PoW environment. As we have seen, the foundational model discussed by Mantovi, and Arnosti, and Weinberg, provides sharp elements for interpreting concentration, but cannot represent a satisfactory account of the complexities involved. In fact, Arnosti and Weinberg have subsequently upgraded their discussion, building a picture of the vertical structure of the industry and of the economies of scope therein. The model developed by Arnosti and Weinberg (2022)—that enlarges the reach of the article published in the proceedings of the ITCS—is an ideal setting to start with for appreciating in which sense the basic mining game represents the foundation of the game theoretic inquiry on PoW.

The Authors address the vertical structure of the industry as stylized by the interaction of production and ownership of mining equipment. Empirical evidence about concentration in specialized hardware production has been collected, in primis concerning the role of market leader of Bitmain. This empirical target is part of the inspiration of the analytical structure of model, which combines a Cournot-like competition in mining with a Bertrand competition in the sale of specialized hardware. Mirroring the basic game, players are represented as homogeneous, to the extent that they share the same strategic space, but this time are differentiated not only by the operational costs of mining but also by the hardware costs of producing specialized equipment. The model is a two-stage game whose payoffs represent the sum of profits coming from selling hardware in the first stage (resulting in deterministic revenues) and from operating equipment in the second stage (resulting in stochastic rewards).

The first stage of the game features miners competing on price for the sale of specialized hardware and deciding whether or not to mine for themselves. The assumption of Bertrand competition manifests the instrumental (in the sense of Samuelson) character of the model. Recall that price competition is typically connected with the homogeneity (lack of differentiation) of the marketed product. However, in the model under consideration, Bertrand competition is primarily meant to shape the strategic space and payoff profile of players, so that each of them finds it profitable to lower price by a sufficiently small amount, since market shares and profits are continuous functions of such price, whereas sales make finite jumps. Furthermore, a player may content himself with selling hardware and not engage in mining, once not in a position to exploit operational cost advantages. These are strong intuitions about the generic equilibrium with sales, which manifest what "art" is employed in the elaboration of the model.

A crucial feature of the model is that players are not subject to capacity constraints, that is, they are in a position to supply whatever amount of hardware the market demands. This is evidently an assumption that is not realized in empirical settings, but one should not consider this idealization as a weakness of the model, and rather as an instance of parsimony—and therefore a generality—in the representation of the strategic environment (in a following section we shall encounter capacity constraints).

Arnosti and Weinberg (2022) characterize miners by operational costs OC and hardware costs HC. Mirroring the analysis of the basic game, the Authors sort players in a well-defined order of nondecreasing hardware costs, so that player 1 (perhaps in the company of identical competitors) is the leader in this competitiveness ordering. The economies of scope of vertical integration are stylized by combining hardware costs and operational costs in a simple additive form so that the unit cost for miner i reads

$$c_i = OC_i + HC_i + HC_j$$

with the last term denoting the unit cost of sourcing from another player labelled j. This simple cost structure enhances the readability of the model and facilitates a comparison with the properties of the basic mining game.

In the second stage of the game, the risk-neutral miners engage in a rent-seeking contest that mirrors perfectly the basic mining game. The Authors abandon the convention of unit reward as numeraire, and write R for the fixed reward (again, expected reward for risk-neutral miners), with the consequence that cost functions now have the same dimension of R. Again, the Authors define a function X as (formula 7, ivi)

$$X(c) \equiv \sum_{k=1}^{n} \max\left(1 - \frac{c_k}{c}, 0\right)$$

(we have simplified somewhat the notation so as to facilitate comparison with our formula 3.7) that aggregates the cost competitiveness indices of players, this time featuring costs c_k that aggregate operational costs and hardware costs. Again, the condition $X = 1$ triggers the equilibrium of this competition, and, unsurprisingly, the Authors identify a unique equilibrium strategy profile in quantities/activities (formula 9, ivi) that mirrors our formula (3.8) above. However, this time, the activity profile is contingent on the allocation of hardware capacity. In this sense, a second-stage equilibrium can be considered a mapping from hardware prices to mining activity levels. Then, given one such equilibrium in quantities, one can employ backward induction to identify the subgame perfect equilibrium of the entire game.

We shall comment in a later section on the generality of the backward induction approach to the equilibrium selection problem. For the moment it matters to emphasize that, in line with the methodology of industrial economics, the sequential structure of the game form does not represent a sequence of dates, but a hierarchy of strategic nodes. And here we come to the emergence of vertical integration.

In principle, three types of equilibria can exist in the model developed by Arnosti and Weinberg (2022), namely, equilibria (I) in which player 1 sells hardware and engages in mining, equilibria (II) in which player 1 sells hardware and chooses not to mine, and equilibria (III) in which player 1 does engage in mining and sells nothing. It is the exogenous parameters of the model that trigger the occurrence of such different situations, in ways that Arnosti and Weinberg (2022) pin down in a series of theorems.

Suppose player 1 is the sole leader, i.e. $HC_1 < HC_2$. Then, Theorem 2 establishes that there is always an equilibrium with sales in which player 1 sets a price in the interval $[HC_1, HC_2]$ and produces all hardware. This equilibrium reflects the essence of the baseline Bertrand equilibrium; further results are needed to characterize the occurrence of different types of equilibria.

Theorem 3 establishes that in an equilibrium in which sales occur, player 1 either charges the highest price HC_2 that guarantees a monopolistic position or sets a lower price in the interval (HC_1, HC_2) and does not mine. Intuition for this result is that it is the entry threshold of participating in the equilibrium in activities, much like in the basic game, that triggers the decision of player 1 of whether or not to mine; in other words, the decision to mine hinges on p_1, that gauges the part of profits coming from selling hardware. The Authors notice that in case $p_1 < HC_2$, player 1 may earn higher profits by switching to the strategy of setting $p_1 = HC_2$ and committing not to mine, but this strategy is not part of the game form under consideration—and, after all, one may question the credibility of one such commitment in the Bitcoin ecology.

Then, Theorem 4 characterizes equilibria with no sales in terms of a triple of conditions. First, inactive miners have weakly higher hardware costs than active miners. Second, if at least three miners are active in equilibrium, inactive miners have strictly higher operational costs than active miners. Third, if active miners do not have identical hardware costs, there is an inactive miner that would profitably mine by using hardware from any active player.

These situations invite us to argue about the generality of these equilibria. The Authors consider three types of deviation from an equilibrium with no sales (recall, a Nash equilibrium is one in which no unilateral deviation is profitable), namely (a) an inactive miner sells hardware to an active one, (b) an inactive miner sells hardware to an inactive one, and (c) an active miner sells hardware to another active one. These deviations can be considered in their explicit consequences on payoffs, among which the fact that in an equilibrium with no sales, low operational costs imply competitive hardware costs, or the existence of an inactive miner with low enough operational cost to source from any other miner. In this sense, equilibria with sales can be considered not generic.

Interestingly, the Authors provide a numerical example (Example 1, ivi) of an equilibrium without sales that sheds light on the way the distribution of competitiveness among players drives the emergence of equilibrium outcomes.

It is not our task to reproduce the proofs of the above theorems, and we refer the reader to the original paper. True, building on our analysis of the basic mining game, we can elaborate as follows.

The aggregate level of activity s (the global hashrate) is the pivot of our approach. In the previous chapter, we have been elaborating on the consequences of the analytic insight that $m = 1/s$, which enables us to write the function X in terms of $\max(1 - sc_k, 0)$, and, as a consequence, equilibrium profiles and entry thresholds. This practice may shed further light on the generality of the discussion by Arnosti and Weinberg (2022), in particular concerning the occurrence of different types of equilibria. Furthermore, our in-and-out-of-equilibrium discussion of Chapter 3 may provide elements for refining such a picture.

4.2.1 *The Interpretation of the Selection Rule*

Evidence that miners operate at full capacity has been repeatedly reported. One may find this evidence not that surprising; after all, the high cost of specialized hardware leads one to suppose that levels of installed capacity are typically chosen accurately. Can one consider the model discussed in this section as a recipe for discussing such choices? This is a challenging question that we have no ambition to answer; the following remarks can be considered preliminary intuitions about what it means to address one such question.

Operating mining equipment at varying intensity (hash rates) *rationally*, by definition, means having contingent plans that reflect the properties of a model game of the environment. To our knowledge, such plans do not seem to have been the subject of systematic discussions in blogs and forums. It seems that operating at full capacity is sort of standard practice. Well, the model by Arnosti and Weinberg (2022) can be considered a picture in which operating at full capacity is subsumed in the game form, in that it is installed computational capacity that enters the selection rule adopted in the paper.

Recall, in Chapter 3 the Bitcoin selection rule has been discussed in its mathematical properties, with due attention to dimensional consistency, but leaving physical units of activity levels unspecified. In this section, on the other hand, the specification of levels as capacity installed shapes a normative discussion of the vertical structure of the industry. Part of this structure is exogenously assumed, like the fact that each miner can be a hardware producer as well. Endogenous features of this structure emerge as general equilibria, in particular a type of vertical integration in which production is concentrated in the hands of the most efficient player.

Thus, the Bitcoin selection rule can represent both instantaneous levels of activity and levels of installed capacity. However, for miners operating at full capacity, the global hashrate remains the pivotal degree of freedom at play.

The conclusions of the above model invite different representations of the vertical structure of the market. In the following section we address one such model.

4.3 Investment in State-of-the-Art Hardware

The vertical structure of the Bitcoin industry is also the subject of Capponi et al. (2022) and this paper is an interesting counterpart to the one we have been discussing in the previous section. The Authors tailor a model that features investment in state-of-the-art hardware and mining decisions, and thereby closely resembles the approach of Arnosti and Weinberg (2022). Still, Capponi et al. (2022) make no room for vertical integration and elaborate on the implications of capacity constraints for the analysis of mining activity; in doing so, the Authors target strategic forces that promote decentralization.

To begin with, Capponi et al. (2022) acknowledge evidence that hardware manufacturers do not seem to be largely involved in mining activity. A number of large producers of specialized hardware state an official policy of not engaging in self-mining. Further evidence concerns the short supply of specialized hardware, which may take months for delivery, and that invites a theoretical investigation of its consequences. One may notice differences with the premises of Arnosti and Weinberg (2022) but should not look for contradiction. The mining industry is in its nascent period and is rapidly evolving, and actual patterns do not reflect an equilibrium that one can consider a consolidated economic structure. In fact, the emerging economic models of the mining industry are exactly meant to provide hints about *how* the industry may evolve toward *what* structures. In this sense, the apparent contradiction between these papers is in fact a hint of the richness of the problem at hand, for which the final word is currently out of reach.

Capponi et al. (2022) model a game whose first stage features miners investing in state-of-the-art computational resources. The Authors employ the Greek letter β to denote the cost components pertaining to investment in state-of-the-art hardware, and the letter η for adjustment costs. A second stage follows in which miners choose activity levels under capacity constraints.

Much like in the paper by Arnosti and Weinberg (2022), the second stage of the game resembles the basic game among risk-neutral miners. Capponi et al. (2022) fix the equilibrium condition for which marginal revenue equals marginal cost in formula 4.1, which corresponds to our FOC (3.2) of Chapter 3. As expected, this second stage admits a unique subgame equilibrium in which the active miners are the more cost-competitive, and the more the competitiveness, the larger the activity share. Again, at least two miners are active in equilibrium. However, this time, miners are restricted in their ability to acquire new hardware.

In fact, much like in the model discussed in the previous section, the equilibrium strategy profile of this second stage is contingent on the investment level, which is the subject of the first stage of the game. Again, backward induction enables one to identify an equilibrium in the first stage of the game. The Authors fix these equilibrium conditions in Sect. 5 (ivi) and establish the natural property that investment decreases for increasing adjustment costs. The Authors identify an interesting approximation scheme in which the investment profile is determined by a set of linear equations, whose coefficients are the partial derivatives of payoff functions with respect to the βs for vanishing β.

In order to investigate the impact of investment on mining, Capponi et al. (2022) parametrize adjustment costs so as to account for possible heterogeneity across miners. For negligible heterogeneity, investment reduces the disparity in hash rates. Then, beyond a certain threshold, investment increases the gap between small and large miners. With that said, the investment stage is a stage of *strategic substitution* to the extent that the investment of one miner generates a negative externality (we already know, generated by the linear aggregative property of the rent-seeking game) on competitors.

It is interesting that the endogenous properties of the model enlighten elements of decentralization that deviate from the conclusions of Arnosti and Weinberg (2022). Among other things, the equilibria identified by Capponi et al. (2022) feature large enough miners (a scale effect) reducing their hash rate as other miners become less efficient. This is one of the results that may be further investigated in connection with our results on the link between the functions X and Υ (see Chapter 3).

In our view, the comparison between the assumption and implications of the two above papers provides general lines of reasoning for the strategic analysis of PoW, in the first instance concerning different interpretations of the selection rule, and the correspondingly different effects triggered by levels of installed capacity or varying rates of activity. In this sense, these two models are not competing descriptions of the Bitcoin environment, but rather complementary accounts of different forces that lead to different outcomes—much like models of industrial competition consider different strategies and effects, which are not meant to contradict one another. Capponi et al. (2022) envision effects that prevent overcentralization. Still, this kind of centralization remains in the hands of stylized miners. The following section introduces more realistic degrees of freedom.

4.4 The Implications of Mining Pools

The emergence of mining pools is among the key phenomena that have characterized the short history of PoW thus far. It is a plain fact that the overwhelming majority of Bitcoin mining resources have clustered within and around pools over the last few years, and a substantial consensus ascribes this occurrence to the desirability of risk sharing for smoothing reward profiles. Actual miners face deterministic cost and stochastic reward prospects that may not fit their financial robustness, and therefore have incentives to share resources and expected rewards according to mechanisms that yield smoother payoff profiles. Pools provide one such mechanism: by smoothing rewards, pools provide a liquidity service for which risk-averse miners display a willingness to pay. In this sense, introducing risk-aversion opens a truly relevant economic dimension in the game theory of PoW. One then asks about the implications for decentralization, and in this respect the model developed by Cong et al. (2021) conveys truly sharp insights into the interaction of risk sharing and competition. Let us sketch the essentials of the paper.

In line with Leshno and Strack (2020), Cong et al. (2021) acknowledge the absence of economies of scale in the aggregation of mining resources, as long as risk-neutrality is maintained and the competition does fit the model of the basic mining game. In addition, one notices that the models discussed in the previous sections feature strategic concentration in settings in which risk-neutral miners have multidimensional strategic space, but no aggregation occurs. More elaborate game forms are necessary to introduce risk attitudes and smoothing of payoffs. It is this methodological step that represents the true focus of this section, beyond the fact that the results of Cong et al. (2021) seem to fix robust insights on the economics of pools.

To begin with, the Authors introduce a sharp differentiation of players. On the one hand, one has individual risk-averse active miners facing the problem of allocating computational resources across pools or perhaps engaging in solo mining. One also has passive miners that allocate resources not strategically. Miners are perfectly competitive, in the sense that they are *takers* of pool fees. On the other hand, one has a fixed number of pools already in place that compete to attract miners. Being fee *makers*, pools share market power. By representing pools already in place, the model does not "explain" the emergence of these entities. This should not be considered a weakness of the model; notice that the concrete emergence of pools is not a continuous process like the formation of "islands" in a material undergoing a phase transition, and rather a phenomenon that manifests itself discontinuously with entry in the industry.

A key feature of the model is an exogenous parametrization of "passive" hash rates, i.e. computational power exogenously allocated across pools, that the Authors interpret in terms of inattention or more general sources of inefficiency. Passive hash rates generate market power once pools enjoy a stable fraction of passive customers, with a clear analogy with a stable layer of loyal customers for a company. These passive rates pivot the outcome of the strategic interaction between pools and miners, in that pools are perfect substitutes in offering risk-sharing services, so that, absent frictions, pools charge vanishing fees as the outcome of a Bertrand competition. Passive hash rates are the friction that generates the market power of pools. Furthermore, the existence of passive hash rate enables one to interpret the model in dynamic terms: one can consider the fixed distribution of passive hash rates as the "initial" condition for the strategic dynamics generated by active miners, and in this sense, one can interpret pools as "growing."

In the model, M pools offer proportional-fee contracts, namely, contracts in which a miner pays a fee that is a constant fraction f of the payout (this specific assumption should not be crucial for the qualitative properties of the model) and these participation costs are part of the specification of the strategic problem of active miners. The feasibility of such a contract rests on the fact that miners' hash rates are not unobservable to a pool manager, since one can observe the partial solutions of puzzles attained by miners, and such partial solutions are, on average, a correct measure of applied hash rates.

In line with the previous Authors, Cong et al. (2021) posit a two-stage game in which backward induction isolates the economically interesting equilibrium. In the first stage of the game, pool managers choose what fee rates to charge; in the second stage, a continuum of infinitesimal miners choose the allocation of resources λ across pools. A strategy profile of the game therefore involves a pair of M–tuples $(f_1, \ldots, f_M)$, $(\lambda_1, \ldots, \lambda_M)$; to be precise, game theorists would underscore that a *strategy* for a second mover is a function from the set of first tuples to the set of second tuples.

The first stage of the game features a decisive departure from the basic competition among miners. In fact, Cong et al. (2021) are required to make analytic room for smoothed reward profiles, and this analytical problem is inherently out of the reach of the instantaneous one-shot game we have been discussing in Chapter 3. Therefore, the Authors introduce a time dimension in which miners operate and get rewarded. Recall, the Poisson distribution characterizes stochastic events that occur at a constant rate and is a function of the dimensionless product μT of the rate of occurrence μ and of the length T of the time interval in which the phenomenon is observed. The event that a node successfully hashes a block can be considered to belong in this class.

To begin with, one must compare payoffs from solo mining and joining pools. Consider first the distribution for solo mining, that we write

$$Poisson\left(\frac{T}{D}p_A\right)$$

(compare formula 1 in Cong et al., 2021, in order to facilitate the interpretation of symbols). The variable T denotes the time interval in which miner A operates, and the parameter D denotes the average time interval between block creation; therefore, for integer T/D, this dimensionless ratio equals the number of block rewards that the miner competes for. Then, the variable p_A is the one defined by the Bitcoin selection rule, i.e. the ratio of resources deployed by the miner (that the Authors write λ_A) over the aggregate hashrate (that the Authors write Λ). And here once again one witnesses the foundational role of the basic mining game: the analytical form of the selection rule enters the argument of the reward distribution of risk-averse miners. This is an intuition that readers may want to focus on: the ratio p_A /D (with the correct dimension of inverse time) is the rate of the Poisson distribution, i.e. the rate at which, by chance, the miner happens to find a solution to the cryptopuzzle in place.

One compares the above solo profile with the corresponding figure for miner A participating in pool B, namely

$$\frac{\lambda_A}{\lambda_A + \Lambda_B}\ Poisson\left(\frac{T}{D}p_{A+B}\right)$$

(compare formula 2, ivi) where p_{A+B} measures the share of global resources deployed by A and B together. One can prove that this reward prospect second order stochastically dominates[1] the one from solo mining so that *any* risk-averse miner prefers to join pools.

With this profit prospect, miners engage in allocations across pools. Some formal analogy with previous models remains, to the extent that in the second stage of the game, miners choose the optimal allocation of resources. One can consider first the frictionless limit, i.e. the particular case in which no passive rates are in place, so that pools are forced to charge vanishing fees. In this case, miners are indifferent between allocations, and one can consider the symmetric allocation as the natural equilibrium of the market.

One can then consider the general case of the optimal allocation contingent on the distribution of fee rates and passive hash rates (formula 14, ivi). The equilibrium allocation has the intuitive property that, given identical fee rates, the absolute amount of resources allocated to a pool is proportional to the size of its passive hash rate, and this allocation diminishes with increasing fee rate (Lemma 1, ivi).

Then, backward induction enables one to fix the equilibrium condition for fees. In this equilibrium condition, pool managers take into account the effect of fees on their own pool size, as well as the effect on the global hashrate. The equilibrium fee setting has the intuitive property that larger pools charge a higher fee rate (Proposition 3, ivi), so that larger pools grow slower. The Authors underscore the difference with standard empirical evidence in industrial economics for which size and growth are positively correlated.

All in all, the equilibrium of the system is pivoted by the balance of forces that promote or counter centralization. This point has significant empirical relevance, since "none of the large pools emerged has snowballed into dominance for prolonged periods of time" (ivi). One notices that 51% of hashrate has been reached by GHash.io in July 2014, but the evolution of the environment seems to display a mean reverting momentum of the size of pools. A growing pool is said to generate a "negative externality" on other miners, that in fact boils down to the

[1] One can consider normal distributions of reward with the same mean and different variance in order to grasp intuitively the significance of second order stochastic dominance. Risk-neutral agents are indifferent between the two distributions, whereas risk-averse agents strictly prefer the one with lower variance.

form of linear aggregation represented in the Bitcoin selection rule. The arms race depicted by Cong et al. (2021) is a more articulated representation of the best response pattern of the game that we have discussed in Chapter 3, but again the implications of linear aggregativity manifest the foundational role of the basic mining game.

Among the interesting analytical aspects of the paper one notices the representation of the risk-aversion of miners by means of CARA von Neumann–Morgenstern utility functions, whose factorization properties enable one to simplify the optimization problem of such miners, in that the problem decouples in M problems of allocation in individual pools. In the concluding part of the paper, the Authors consider the potential entry of new pools and find that again pools can charge positive fees, provided passive hash rates remain. The paper also contains a statistical analysis meant to test the positive relevance of the model. The Authors notice that available data do confirm the basic results of the model that larger pools and pools with larger passive hash rates charge higher fees and grow more slowly.

We are not going to reproduce the results of Cong et al. (2021) and refer the reader to the original paper. Let us point out that a major phenomenon represented in the model is that concurring forces may drive mean reverting effects on concentration. The interaction of risk sharing (that promotes centralization) and competition (that promotes decentralization) manifests itself with the fact that, in the words of the Authors, larger pools better internalize their externality on global hash rates, that is, take advantage of their dominant position in the selection rule, and therefore charge higher fees and grow more slowly than smaller pools. Furthermore, the process of centralization of resources in pools may not decisively undermine the decentralization of mining, since miners can reallocate resources across pools with no adjustment costs. It has been even argued that pools, via the liquidity service they provide, may foster decentralization. We invite the reader to look at these far-reaching insights from the methodological standpoint that the global hashrate is again the pivotal degree of freedom at play.

4.5 Users, Miners, and Block Composition

The basic mining game is a contest over the reward of a single block. In this one-shot setting, one is not interested in what exactly a block is. However, the composition of blocks is of great importance for blockchain stakeholders, and therefore for theoretic reasoning. This is the subject of the model developed by Malik et al. (2022). The incentives that counter the growth in Bitcoin throughput are at stake in this model, and the methodological separation between technological and economic aspects becomes an issue in itself. These challenges make the model a stimulating first step toward higher levels of complexity of PoW phenomena. Catalini and Gans (2020) argue that the drivers of growth of a blockchain environment evolve with precise network effects. The effects discussed by Malik et al. (2022) can be considered part of this picture that marks the complexity of the ecology.

Malik et al. (2022) address the strategic forces involved in block composition, starting from a pair of key facts. First, it is well known that there is a technical lower bound (a bottleneck) in the time interval between the addition of new blocks to the ledger, corresponding to the time it takes to reach agreement on the proper continuation of the chain of blocks. Second, somewhat well-documented evidence exists about the practice of partial block filling. This emergent phenomenon is not due to technical factors like the previous one and rather reflects strategic behavior, witness the criticisms that have been raised against AntPool for such behavior. "We will continue mining empty blocks. This is the freedom given by the Bitcoin protocol." This has been the answer to critics. Building on such premises, Malik et al. (2022) elaborate a model game whose equilibria rationalizes the emergence of a significant phenomenology. What follows is a brief sketch of the picture.

4.5.1 Game Form and Key Results

Malik et al. (2022) depict a game between users and miners for block construction. A game tree with two nodes is the core of the game form. In the first node, users decide whether or not to transact via the blockchain, and, in case, what fee to offer. Along this leaf is located the second node, at which miners decide what blocks to create with what pending transactions. One thereby enlarges the strategic space of stylized miners, in order to represent the incentives to validate primarily transactions with higher fees. Thus, the game models the competition among users over fees; one of the goals of the Authors is explain *why* fees exist. Backward induction is employed in the identification of the subgame perfect equilibrium, in which users identify the optimal fee schedule.

The strategy of double-spending is also available to strategic miners. The general traits of such an attack have been extensively discussed in the literature. Malik et al. (2022) devise a refinement of such a strategy that fits the strategic structure under investigation. Larger miners have, on average, a larger share of revenue, in the precise sense shaped by the selection rule. Market power induces large miners to underutilize block capacities to force users into competition on fees. The game is repeated indefinitely. This infinite horizon enables the Authors to introduce punishment mechanisms that generalize those at play in the infinitely repeated prisoners dilemma. Such mechanisms help sustain a collusion equilibrium in which large miners create blocks only partially filled with high-fee transactions.

These are the key features of the model, whose main message is the existence of a fundamental tradeoff between collusion and the security of the network. Collusion overlooks small transactions, whereas double-spending threatens large ones. These strategic forces are the sources that generate the emergence of the phenomena under investigation. As a consequence, the growth potential of Bitcoin throughput is inherently limited by the interactions at play. An interesting implication is that collusion can be seen as beneficial in its incentives to invest in the security of the network.

4.5.2 *Connection with the Basic Mining Game and the Linear Aggregator*

At first sight, the strategic forces represented in the basic mining game seem to be scarcely at play in the above setting. Still, it is the Bitcoin selection rule that gauges the market power of large miners as expected (steady state) share of revenues, and it is to the basic mining game that we must trace the emergence of such an outcome as Nash equilibrium. Users want their transactions validated by miners and then recorded in the immutable chain. To mine partially filled blocks is an option embedded in the Bitcoin protocol: the market power of large miners enables them to force users into competition over fees. To represent large miners exercising such an option as an equilibrium outcome is a major achievement of Malik et al. (2022). In Sect. 2.1 of the paper, the Authors trace the distribution of market power to the skewed distribution of mining hardware and cost efficiency, which we have been tracing to the basic mining game. We are in a position to refine such a remark.

First, Malik et al. (2022) align with a large part of the literature in identifying the endogenous entry condition so that the marginal miner makes a vanishing expected profit. In such a condition the Authors reduce the costs of mining to the single fixed cost of acquiring hardware equipment. Such an analytical simplification is undoubtedly a sound way to sharpen the content of the model; still, the theoretical and empirical relevance of the aggregate scale of mining activity is essentially connected with variable costs, in the senses discussed in the previous chapter. The benchmark m of marginal cost and the aggregate scale s of mining activity are reciprocal, in the sense of our discussion leading to our identity (3.11) of Chapter 3 connecting absolute and relative aggregate best responses. The equilibrium activity level of the basic game is therefore an implicit ingredient of the emergent properties discussed by Malik et al. (2022).

Second, consider the differentiation between passive and strategic miners. The essential rational behavior of passive miners is shaped by the basic game, which is therefore in the background of the picture developed by Malik et al. (2022). On the other hand, strategic miners are endowed with a larger strategic space, which accommodates the option of double-spending. We have pointed out in Chapter 1 that the literature has already discussed the incentives to undertake such an attack; Malik et al. (2022) provide a refined discussion of the payoffs from double-spending in comparison with those of "honest" mining. In this sense of comparison, again, the Nash equilibrium of the basic game inherently underlies a strategic analysis of double-spending.

Third, the level of complexity targeted by Malik et al. (2022) entangles technological and economic aspects of PoW. More payments require more information to be transmitted, and the physical constraints over such processes impinge on the strategic spaces of players. It is well known that there are lower limits to the time interval in which the P2P network can reach consensus over the proper continuation of the chain. With shorter time intervals between blocks, multiple forks may emerge as the P2P nodes do not share enough time to get in sync. Malik et al. (2022) assume away technological effects of information propagation, in order to focus on the strategic nature of the problem under investigation, but admit that computer science and economics superpose in the phenomena under consideration. For instance, a specialized literature has discussed the role of congestion in shaping the conditions for participation in a P2P network; well, Bitcoin miners prefer the increase of congestion of the platform.

4.5.3 *An Instrumental Model*

It goes without saying that our brief account makes no justice of the sophisticated discussion by Malik et al. (2022). Our main goal was to highlight the premises and the objectives of the model, and thereby the extent to which it can be considered instrumental in the sense of Samuelson (2016).

Malik et al. (2022) are somewhat explicit in motivating the various aspects of the game form, for instance, the infinite repetition is functional to the emergence of punishment mechanisms. The insights motivating the model are crucial for its instrumental character, for instance decreasing the difficulty of puzzles may well decrease hashing time but not necessarily increase throughput. Perhaps one proposition can be considered the inspiration of the model: "decentralization and its many facets (number of miners, cumulative mining power, and miner homogeneity) are not simultaneously achievable or even desirable" (ivi, Sect. 2). Evidently, no single model can account for the complexity of the content of the proposition, and different models can be instrumental as complementary representations of the many facets of decentralization.

4.6 Overview

The nascent game theoretic literature on blockchain and PoW already displays an astonishing liveness. Not only do papers emerge at a substantial rate, but display manifold interests in phenomena and strategic assumptions. Liu et al. (2019) provide an overview of the themes that the previous game theoretic literature has been covering. Of the papers that we have been addressing, only the one by Cong et al. (2021) is quoted, albeit as a preprint. Still, this review can be useful in providing a map of the terrain that game theoretic approaches are in a position to cover, which ranges from purely economic analysis to more technically oriented contributions. We refer the reader to Liu et al. (2019) for a rich list of references and inspirations.

It was not our aim to provide a comparable overview of the game theoretic literature on cryptocurrencies. Our ambition is to pin down the *foundations* of the economics of PoW, along the lines depicted by Leshno and Strack (2020) and Mantovi (2021). In this sense, our monograph is meant to contribute to such a literature, albeit with a light touch and a discussant style. It is worth quoting a pair of Authors.

A truly interesting contribution is the paper by Pagnotta (2022), that tailors a model in which the price of Bitcoin interacts with the security of the network. It is well established that the reward from mining has a role in the security of the network; in fact, this is the innovation brought about by Nakamoto. Pagnotta (2022) elaborates on this basic fact and tailors a game between users and miners that displays the relevance of the *security function* of the system. This function characterizes the responsiveness of the system to a malicious attack by fixing the probability that the system survives the attack. Following the Nakamoto (2008) design, given computational resources H and A of honest miners and attackers respectively, this function can be written

$$S(H, A) = \begin{cases} 1 - \left(\frac{A}{H}\right)^k & for \quad A < H \\ 0 & else \end{cases}$$

after a fork has already generated k blocks. This security function influences the forces impinging on the exchange rate of Bitcoin with the reference currency, that is, the currency with which consumers buy goods. The security of the network then emerges as a sophisticated economic equilibrium outcome: "there is no one-to one mapping between technological primitives and the security level: the same fundamentals are compatible with a strongly or a weakly secured payment system. Put simply, one can only assess the security properties of a particular *equilibrium allocation* in a system such as Bitcoin, but not that of its blockchain technology" (ivi).

In the model, the global hashrate is a pivotal degree of freedom, and in this sense, the model does fit our methodological interest in the aggregative nature of the basic mining game. In fact, as already pointed out, this model seems to set the stage for framing the economics and the computer science of consensus and security as complementary approaches, in which endogenous equilibria emerge as game theoretic results. With that said, even a brief sketch of the analytic structure of the paper is beyond our goals, and we refer the reader to the original article.

Another significant paper is the one by Saleh (2021), that is part (as preprint) of the review by Liu et al. (2019). Saleh (2021) addresses the nature of a chain-based Proof-of-Stake (PoS) protocol in terms of a sequential game with infinite periods. It is assumed that at time $t = 0$ a fork occurs. Players are characterized by an initial endowment of coins, are assumed to be risk-neutral, and share the same discount factor δ. The strategy space of players is the direct product of a pair of sets that partition the actions available along each of two branches of the blockchain. In particular, the states in which the branch draws one of the player's coins are characterized; that being the case, the player can either add or not add a block to the branch. The Author defines two strategies in particular, one that reflects the scope of the Longest Chain Rule, and the other reflecting the spirit of the Nothing-at-Stake problem. The Author establishes a number of conditions under which consensus emerges.

To provide a brief sketch of the model is beyond our aim (we refer the reader to the original article), but we consider it relevant to notice that even for PoS a game theoretic literature is emerging, and that within a few years the economic analysis of PoW and PoS may attain comparable advancement, and therefore admit cross-fertilization of research contributions.

4.7 Emergent Phenomena and Equilibrium Selection

The models of the previous sections shed light on significant traits of the physiology of PoW. Beyond the specific realm to which models have been applied, however, it matters to appreciate the methodological steps involved in the discussion. Starting with the seminal short paper by Philip Warren Anderson (1972), the *more is different* paradigm has been progressively acknowledged as a pillar of the modern science of complexity. According to this paradigm, scientific representations of different layers of reality make "jumps," in which new variables and principles emerge, that can be *reduced* to those of the underlying level (think of reducing biological phenomena to the underlying chemical processes) but cannot be *constructed* out of them. Social scientists are displaying increasing interest in this hierarchy of complexity.

For instance, Gintis (2009) argues that game theory offers a unique language for the potential unification of behavioral sciences (biology, psychology, anthropology, sociology, economics, political science), on account of its ability to represent different levels of strategic complexity. We have been exposed to such different levels in this and the preceding chapter. Cong et al. (2021) explicitly acknowledge the Bitcoin industrial organization as a unique social science laboratory into which to put our analytical models at work. This "uniqueness" can be related to the short history of cryptocurrencies, and with the fact that the environment is rapidly evolving. It is the aim of this section to focus on the methodological point that the models discussed in the previous sections have been addressed in terms of ***backward induction***, a solution concept that deserves at least a brief discussion.

4.7.1 The Limits of Backward Induction

The limits of backward induction as an equilibrium selection device represent a well-developed theme among game theorists (see Binmore, 2007; Gintis, 2009) that, though, may not be easily accessible to a more general audience. It may prove useful then to review a few basic ideas about the pros and cons of backward induction.

Clear insights about the limits of backward induction can be conveyed via the simplest form of the ultimatum game, which goes as follows. Consider a noncooperative two-stage game in which two players can split a sum of money according to the following mechanism. Player A offers a split of the sum; then, player B responds by either accepting or refusing the offer. If B accepts, the sum is effectively split as accepted; otherwise, both players get nothing. Players are not supposed to interact again, nor the outcome of the game is supposed to become public information of any sort.

As is well known, the equilibrium selected by rational individualism and backward induction posits that a rational player B prefers any tiny amount of money to nothing. Knowing that, player A offers the tiniest fraction possible, B accepts, and player A gets (substantially) the whole pie. It is well documented that this "rational" outcome has been repeatedly rejected by experiments. Participants typically display a strong sense of fairness, and splits occur with offers around 40%. Thus, a major flaw of backward induction approaches concerns potential conflicts with social norms (like fairness) that may frame a specific strategic interaction within a larger behavioral setting. With that said, there is a limit in which the problem assumes different dimensions. Is there a threshold of decoupling between rationality and fairness?

Splitting a sum of money, prima facie, is a problem of relative allocations, and the ***ordinal*** nature of payoffs makes the problem 1-dimensional, i.e. characterized by the single variable "ratio of shares." Still, one can enlarge the problem and consider ***cardinal*** payoffs, which can parametrize wealth (level) effects that may pivot empirical outcomes. For instance, if the sum to be split is a trillion dollar, each of us, playing the second mover, would gladly accept a tiny 1% share of the pie, since this would have impressive consequences on our wealth. In a nutshell, in the limit of large-level effects, the problem of the fairness of the offer mitigates significantly (possibly, evaporates) and backward induction regains its traction. We refer to Binmore (2007) for a review of the multiple equilibria of the ultimatum game that are not selected by backward induction arguments.

Another stimulating example of the limits of backward induction is given by the surprise examination game (that some refer to as the *hanging paradox*; see Gintis, 2009, p. 105). A professor announces that a surprise written exam will occur one day of the next week. Among the students are a pair of bold backward inductors that get excited from the perspective of solving the puzzle. They argue that the exam cannot evidently take place on Friday, since no surprise would then occur. Then, with Friday eliminated from the choice set, the exam cannot take place on Thursday as well, for the same reason. Following this line of argument, the bold inductors reason that there is no surprise day in the next week. Backward induction indicates that the exam cannot be given. There is a problem with applying backward induction to surprise events.

This paradox has been thoroughly scrutinized. The days of the next week all belong to the same information set that students share as the source of contingency in their strategic responses (say, maximize effort immediately in order to be ready on Monday, balance the effort with potential other allocations of time, etc.). The above backward inductors have been reasoning backward in time (from Friday to Thursday and so on) but not backward in the strategic tree of the game. Therefore, they have not been using backward induction in the proper sense. Furthermore, on intuitive grounds, one notices some "analogy" with the way backward induction identifies the unique subgame perfect equilibrium of the repeated prisoners dilemma in which players always defect, a prediction that is largely considered unsound, and is in fact rejected by experimental evidence. Overall, one is invited to caution about the general applicability of selection devices. We refer to Gintis (2009) for a comprehensive discussion of rationalizability and backward induction.

Albeit acknowledging the intellectual stimuli coming from these considerations, some readers may question their relevance for the truly concrete properties of PoW. This is a good question that deserves a few remarks. The saying goes among game theorists that everything looks like a nail to a baby with a hammer. It is tempting to use a device that is known to work fine to find a solution to any problem that comes in the way, and it can be appealing to devise two-stage games that one knows at the outset can be "solved" (in the sense that an equilibrium can be selected) via backward induction. Still, the relevance of such models rests on the conceptual soundness of the methodology applied in the specific setting. It seems useful to recall that economic models (and model games in particular) are not meant to predict empirical outcomes, and rather to represent maps of the incentives at play and, therefore, of the possible outcomes selected by concrete interactions at play. The fundamental questions raised by the equilibrium selection problem are at stake.

Well, one should not interpret these considerations as undermining the consistency of models that use backward induction as equilibrium selection device. On the contrary, these considerations are meant to sharpen the nature of the backward induction device, and therefore the generality of the equilibria thereby selected. For which kind of strategic problems can one consider backward induction a plausible and insightful approach? For sure the models discussed in this chapter fall under this category; the sequential setting and the backward reasoning reflect well-established methods in industrial economics concerning the allocation of strategic power: "first mover" advantage is not in essence a question of sequential moves. How about reversing the sequence of choices? Does it make sense, in some limit or concerning definite aspects, to have pool managers respond to the heterogeneous allocation patterns of individual miners? This can be a way to allocate market power to individual miners, or some other strategic advantage that the evolving phenomenology may display in the future. This kind of exercise is typical among physicists, who love to explore the universe of potential models in order to build intuition on where mathematics can lead you.

A somewhat controversial application of backward induction has been employed for envisioning a potential disruption of the Bitcoin ecology, should mining activity fall behind a critical threshold. A single entity may take control of the majority of hashing power and reorganize balances at will. The integrity of the ledger would be compromised. Then, according to some columnists, a simple application of backward induction teaches us that without the intervention of a group of motivated stakeholders, the new phase would induce the "smart money" to exit the stage. The argument certainly has a point, but our brief methodological focus on backward induction invites us to caution about the certainty that smart money would reason backward from the disintegration of the network to the trigger of an exit option.

4.7.2 Evolution and Coordination

Evolution has a role in equilibrium selection. Evolution manifests itself in the progressive selection of the equilibria that emerge in the real world. The complexity of these processes is among the challenges facing researchers. In such respects, Gintis (2009) provides sharp considerations that deserve explicit quote.

"The evolutionary dynamics of human groups has produced *social norms* that coordinate the strategic interaction of rational individuals and regulate kinship, family life, the division of labor, property rights, cultural norms, and social conventions" (Gintis, 2009, p. 163). In such a perspective, the paradigm of decentralized consensus can perhaps be considered a social norm clustering strong ideals about fairness and equality that have a long history, and that recent technological and conceptual advances have regenerated into seemingly more sustainable architectures. Within such architectures, coordination does matter. For sure the short but noticeable history of cryptocurrencies manifests challenging features that call for sophisticated coordination mechanisms for a proper interpretation. It has been argued that a PoS protocol is superior to PoW, being stakes involved in the validation mechanism. Discussing this superiority in terms of explicit coordination mechanisms seems to represent an insightful line of research on the potentialities of decentralized consensus.

In addition, readers may find it challenging to acknowledge the potential unification of behavioral sciences as a future theoretical background for framing the analysis of blockchain. As pointed out by Gintis (2009), economists and sociologists adopt different methodologies in their interpretation of social phenomena. A large body of economics represents agents and entities as selfish utility/profit maximizers, whereas sociologists depict people as other-regarding moral agents who care about social norms and ethical principles. Well, these different methodologies are not incompatible, and we align with Gintis in arguing that a theoretical framework encompassing both traditions may represent a platform for progress in social sciences. In fact, this vision can provide useful insights into the monetary problem of digital money that we address in the following chapters. Money is a social convention that builds on coordination.

References

Anderson P. W. (1972). More is different. Science 177 (4047), 393–396.

Arnosti N., Weinberg M. (2022). Bitcoin: a natural oligopoly. Management Science 68 (7), 4755–4771.

Binmore K. (2007). Playing for Real. Oxford University Press.

Capponi A., Olaffson S., Alsabah H. (2022). Proof-of-Work cryptocurrencies: does mining technology undermine decentralization? Management Science. Forthcoming.

Catalini C., Gans J. (2020). Some simple economics of the blockchain. Communications of the ACM 63 (7), 80–90.

Cong L. W., He Z., Li J. (2021). Decentralized mining in centralized pools. Review of Financial Studies 34, 1191–1235.

Gintis H. (2009). The Bounds of Reason. Princeton University Press.

Leshno J. D., Strack P. (2020). Bitcoin: an axiomatic approach and an impossibility theorem. American Economic Review: Insights 2 (3), 269–286.

Liu Z., Luong N. C., Wang W., Niyato D., Wang P., Liang Y. C., Kim D. I. (2019). A survey on blockchain: a game theoretical perspective. IEEE Access 7, 47615–47643.

Malik N., Aseri M., Singh P. V., Srinivasan, K. (2022). Why Bitcon will fail to scale? Management Science 68 (10), 7323–7349.

Mantovi A. (2021). Bitcoin selection rule and foundational game theoretic representation of mining competition. Working Paper EP-02. Dipartimento di Scienze Economiche e Aziendali, Parma. Italy. IDEAS/RePEc.

Nakamoto S. (2008). Bitcoin: a peer-to-peer electronic cash system.

Pagnotta E. S. (2022). Decentralizing money: Bitcoin prices and blockchain security. Review of Financial Studies 35, 866–907.

Saleh F. (2021). Blockchain without waste: Proof-of-Stake. Review of Financial Studies 34, 1156–1190.

Samuelson L. (2016). Game theory in economics and beyond. Journal of Economic Perspectives 30 (4), 107–130.

References

[illegible] Science 12[illegible] 346.
[illegible] (20[illegible]) [illegible]
[illegible] 60 4[illegible] 441.
Brennan [illegible] (2007) [illegible] Bail, O. [illegible]
Cappelli, A., Gallego [illegible] M., [illegible] H. (20[illegible]) [illegible] Work [illegible] training technologies and [illegible] Management [illegible]
[illegible]
Catalini C., Gans J. (2020). Some simple economics of the blockchain. Communications of the ACM 63(7), 80–90.
Cong L. W., [illegible] (2021). Decentralized [illegible] Review of Financial Studies 34, 1192–1235.
[illegible] H. (2009). The Bounds of Reason. Princeton University Press.
[illegible] J. D., [illegible] (2020). [illegible] and [illegible] theory. [illegible] Review [illegible]
[illegible] D., Wang [illegible]
(2017). A survey of blockchain: a game theoretical perspective. [illegible]
[illegible]
Malik N., [illegible] (2022). [illegible] Management Science 68, 10[illegible]
Marinoff [illegible] and [illegible] games [illegible] Working Paper [illegible]
Springer [illegible]
Nakamoto S. (2008). Bitcoin: a peer-to-peer electronic cash system.
[illegible] Bitcoin prices [illegible] blockchain [illegible] 36, 895–907.
[illegible] (2021) [illegible] Review of Financial [illegible]
[illegible] 1150–1190.
[illegible]

CHAPTER 5

The Future Monetary System

Abstract This chapter deals with the monetary system as the institutional framework governed by central banks. Central banks provide a public good that no private blockchain can rival. Institutional economics and historical perspectives are natural complements of the theoretical principle of "no questions asked" in framing the problem of the way monetary innovations should be made to fit the existing landscape. In particular, the principle shapes a fundamental tradeoff that impinges on the issuers of stablecoins and, virtually, on any financial intermediary. We sketch the prospect for the future monetary system depicted by the Bank for International Settlements. The Libra/Diem case study is given due emphasis. Stablecoins are given a clear characterization; in particular, it is discussed in which sense there is much more to stablecoins than problems of proper collateralization. The inherent hierarchy of account-based money is the proper setting for tackling these issues. Then, the subtle case for central bank digital currency is thoroughly discussed.

Keyword Institutions · Monetary System · Free Banking Era · Stablecoin · Central Bank Digital Currency

A. Schianchi and A. Mantovi, *The Economics of Cryptocurrencies and Digital Money*, Palgrave Studies in Financial Services Technology, https://doi.org/10.1007/978-3-031-44248-3_5

In the first part of the monograph we have developed our game theoretic approach to the physiology of PoW within a blockchain. This second part of the monograph addresses the broader financial arena and the potential role of new digital coins in the future monetary system. The global monetary system is part and parcel of the macroeconomic and geopolitical framework, and its response to recent digital innovations has been the subject of intense policy analysis over the last decade. Policymakers are continuously refining projections of what a new panorama *should* look like, and what role therein a central bank digital currency (CBDC) can be reasonably expected to play. This is a normative problem in which economic and legal questions are inherently entangled. Part of the participants in the crypto ecology share a kind of "anonymity" that is connected with evading authentication of identity, perhaps aiming at avoiding prosecutability. It is somewhat evident that this feature of the crypto world is not compatible with an advanced institutional setting. On the other hand, the digital innovations that have recently been expanding the technological frontier (whether blockchain-based or not) can represent sound lines of evolution of the monetary system. This is the subject of this chapter.

Compared with previous chapters, this part of the monograph shall develop more qualitative arguments, without equations fixing equilibrium conditions, and with the monetary principle of "no questions asked" (NQA) as the theoretical cornerstone. This should not be considered to lessen the rigor of arguments; after all, economic models do matter to the extent that they represent sound insights. A sharp example is a subtle tradeoff[1] facing the issuer of a stablecoin that goes as follows (see Gorton and Zhang 2023).

On the one hand, the issuer of the stablecoin wants the public to trust the quality of the assets that back the value of the coin and has incentives to release detailed information thereof. On the other hand, as we have seen in Chapter 2, transparency comes at the cost of information sensitivity and therefore potentially emerging panic and runs; therefore, the same issuer may want to maintain opacity about the properness of the collateralization employed, and thereby target a steady state of NQA. This is an inescapable tradeoff that, notice, is not specific to stablecoin issuers, and rather impinges virtually on every financial intermediary (still,

[1] Recall that a tradeoff, albeit expressed in qualitative terms, is a construct that parallels the aim of an equilibrium condition expressed in analytic terms and shares the same level of rigor.

standard textbooks do not seem to emphasize the relevance of this conundrum). We want readers to focus immediately on the generality of these insights, which provide substantial motivation for building a sophisticated monetary vision on digital innovations and coin proliferation. To a large extent, one such vision is independent of the technologies involved. Computer scientists may already appreciate the richness of the conceptual problem facing monetary economists and find stimuli to deepen the subject matter. One more insight concerns coordination.

Game theorists have gone a long way in establishing the relevance of coordination in equilibrium selection problems, and in providing analytical arguments showing why it is often the case that it takes a "choreographer" to guide a system toward a desirable equilibrium (see for instance Gintis 2009). The recent policies of "forward guidance" adopted by major central banks witness the relevance of having strategies in place that prove effective in clustering the attention and the operations of market participants around a prospect equilibrium path that combines desirability and sustainability. Definitely, coordination and institutions are the keywords of this chapter. Coordination in the upgrading of the international monetary system is the persistent focus of international institutions like the Bank for International Settlements. "Money is a coordination device that serves society through its strong network effects" (BIS 2022).

The short history of the phenomena under inquiry and the worries of regulators provide the rationale for our attention to the shortcomings of recent digital innovations. It is relevant for policymakers to anticipate whether pathologies may generate from the disordered proliferation of new digital tokens (witness the crypto downfall of 2022), and it is relevant to rapidly tame stablecoins. This is the uncompromising attitude that we inherited from the great financial crisis of 2007–2009.

5.1 Digital Innovations and Evolving Institutions

It is often the case that financial innovation generates excitement and extraordinary expectations about future scenarios. This has been the case with the promises of DeFi to revolutionize finance. On institutional grounds, however, excitement has little relevance. What matters is the reliability of the financial-monetary system through which private and public endeavors, in both developed and underdeveloped economies, channel funds and payments. The institutional perspective on the crypto/DeFi revolution, therefore, envisions technological breakthroughs as ways to *upgrade* current arrangements, at the same time allowing private profit-seeking entities to exploit their cutting-edge competitiveness within an ordered level playing field. It is a matter of regulation, to which the following chapter is dedicated. Noticeably, at times, "lawmakers are so focused on understanding a new technological innovation that they fail to ask what exactly is being created" (Gorton and Zhang 2023). This is the subject of the present chapter.

A disordered growth of the monetary system is what policymakers are in the first instance committed to preventing. The design of scenarios in which innovations can smoothly enter a well-functioning monetary system is therefore of utmost interest. Here is a picture of the essential elements of a modern payment system, in which the Nonbank represents the "place" that digital innovations (whether blockchain-based or not) can claim.

No wonder, Fig. 5.1 depicts a hierarchy of monetary institutions with the central bank at the apex that provides the public goods (the technical infrastructure and the clearing, settlement, and backstop services) that support the smooth functioning of (and therefore the trust in) the circuit. This is exactly the circuit (and the type of trust) that Bitcoin is meant to circumvent. On the other hand, a number of stablecoins may claim the role of the above Nonbank, provided the structural flaws of cryptocurrencies (the lack of a nominal anchor for price, the limits to scalability, and the lack of regulation of crypto intermediaries) can be fixed. Stablecoins, in principle, may find their way into the picture, provided adequate institutional backing (regulation) and liquidity support can be guaranteed.

We have seen in Chapter 2 in which sense the contemporary monetary problem is at its roots a problem of safe assets and liquidity management along the hierarchy of account-based money. This is in fact the perspective of the BIS (2022) on the map of the desirable properties of the future monetary system. The key potential innovation currently under inquiry is the introduction of a central bank digital currency (CBDC).

Recall, the hierarchy of money has the central bank at the top that issues base money in the form of banknotes (physical cash) that circulate, and bank reserves that generate the chain of account-based money. Physical cash represents "retail" money, in the sense that it is typically used

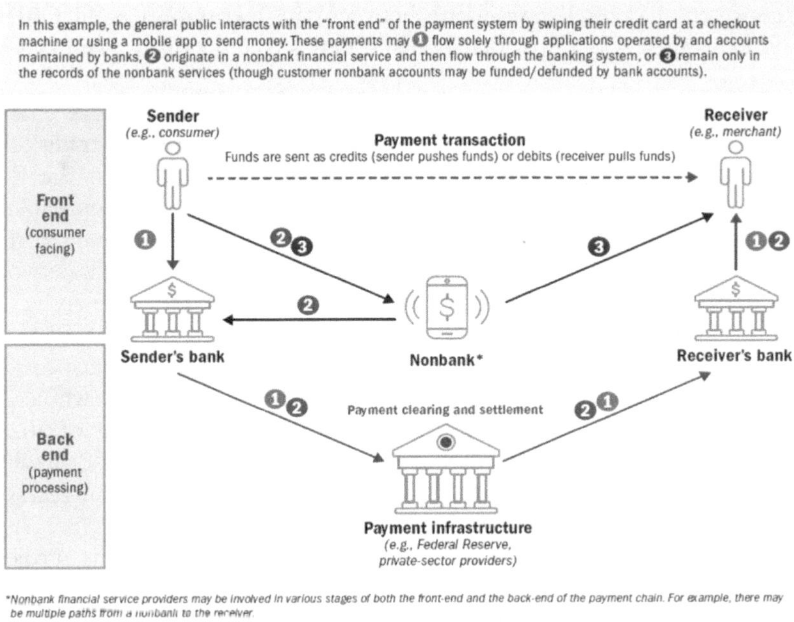

Fig. 5.1 A stylized representation of an advanced payment system. Reproduced from the Board of Governors of the Federal Reserve System (2022)

to buy retail goods and services, whereas bank reserves can be considered "wholesale" money, in the sense of being the source of flows in the monetary system, starting with the loans channeled through the hierarchy of money. Well, the potential of CBDC as well is conjectured to unfold in both retail and wholesale dimensions.

A CBDC can be defined as a digital liability of the central bank meant to be widely available to the general public (Board of Governors of the Federal Reserve System 2022). At the retail level, a CBDC may enable consumers and firms to access directly a safe instrument that enables recent digital innovations to unfold their potential in connection with extant private providers of financial services and their ability to exploit the Application programming interface[2] (API) technology. The BIS (2022)

[2] Application programming interfaces are sets of specifications that improve the communication and interaction between different types of software.

Report emphasizes the similarity between the merits of a retail CBDC and existing services provided by bank deposits and private platforms in general.

In turn, a wholesale CBDC may offer new capabilities and enable transactions between financial intermediaries that bypass the traditional medium of bank reserves. These new capabilities concern in the first instance the technical possibilities of programmability and composability of transactions. However, from the monetary point of view, what matters is the way in which the wholesale dimension may generate new network connections beyond those already in place within the hierarchy of money. This is a truly delicate and controversial question. The Bank of England does witness interest in both retail and wholesale perspectives for the would-be digital pound. The ECB is exploring the wholesale option. A plan for trials, meant to start in the second quarter of 2024, involves commercial participants and the Deutsche Bundesbank providing a trigger payment option such that a private DLT network can access a "Trigger Chain" and thereby the RTGS system.

Technical experimentation is under way. An example is Project Hamilton, a joint effort of the Federal Reserve Bank of Boston and the Massachusetts Institute of Technology, that aims to explore the design space for a CBDC and gain a hands-on understanding of technical challenges, for instance concerning complex functionalities like auditability and programmability. In Phase 1 of the project, a pair of architectures have been tested. A first architecture processes transactions through a server that materializes an ordered transaction history, with a peak throughput of roughly 170,000 transactions per second. A second parallel architecture yields higher throughput (1.7 million transactions per second) but does not materialize an ordered history.

This evolving scenario is filled with challenging technical details that, though, may obscure the fundamental economic dimension underlying, that does not reduce to the economics of information security. It is important to recognize that the design of the future monetary system is a problem in Institutional Economics. Part of the readers may be scarcely familiar with this theoretical perspective and may enjoy a quote from a leading scholar of the field.

"Institutions are the humanly devised constraints that structure political, economic and social interaction. They consist of both informal constraints (sanctions, taboos, customs, traditions, and codes of conduct) and formal rules (constitutions, laws, property rights). Throughout history, institutions have been devised by human beings to create order and reduce uncertainty in exchange. Together with the standard constraints of economics they define the choice set and therefore determine transaction and production costs and hence the profitability and feasibility of engaging in economic activity. They evolve incrementally, connecting the past with the present and the future; history in consequence is largely a story of institutional evolution in which the historical performance of economies can only be understood as part of a sequential story [...] Effective institutions raise the benefits of cooperative solutions or the cost of defection, to use game theoretic terms. In transaction cost terms, institutions reduce transaction and production costs per exchange so that the potential gains from trade are realizable. Both political and economic institutions are essential parts of an effective institutional matrix [...] economic history is overwhelmingly a story of economies that failed to produce a set of economic rules of the game (with enforcement) that induce sustained economic growth" (North 1991). The great financial crisis of 2007–2009 and the role of major central banks (in particular the Federal Reserve) in preventing the collapse of the entire financial system provide empirical lessons about the relevance of institutions.

Practitioners of blockchain operation may wonder whether such a theoretical perspective may display some grip on the concrete implications of DeFi. This is definitely the case. In the Appendix to Chapter 2, we have seen that the historical debate between chartalists and metallists provides clear insights into the problem of money as an inherently institutional problem, which, in turn, displays concrete implications for market design.

For instance, to reduce the monetary problem of stablecoins to a problem of proper collateralization is a myopia—that one may call the "metallist view" of stablecoins—that simply ignores the concrete environment that a stablecoin is supposed to inhabit. Among other things, one must consider the contingent market liquidity of the securities meant to perform the collateralization, the soundness of the concrete network of dealers making markets for those securities, and, last but not least, the regulatory problem of what entities should be chartered issuers of stablecoins. These are major issues involved in the problem of trust in a stablecoin, that is inherently a problem of distributed consensus (to quote an expression that can be interpreted in manifold ways) not within the native blockchain, but in a larger network in which coordination mechanisms are pivotal. This is inherently an institutional problem.

The history of money provides cogent backing for the institutional perspective. For instance, historians have documented the significant monetary consequences of the fall of the Roman Empire. The weakening of governments reflected in a lower quality of their currencies and in a reduced acceptability in commerce, which partially reverted to barter. Well, sharp analogies with the phenomena we are interested in pertain to the free banking era of the nineteenth-century US, when a number of regional banks were allowed to issue their own banknotes, once appropriately backed by national debt securities. The analogy with stablecoins is a sharp one, and one learns straight lessons from this historical episode.

To begin with, those banks were not happy to allocate high-quality securities to the collateralization of banknotes, which were therefore issued in short supply. An explosion of deposits occurred, with a consequential increase in the fragility of the same deposits. This phenomenon manifests the general theme that the relative proportions of monetary aggregates do matter; they did matter in the nineteenth century, and still they matter in the twenty-first. Additional insights conveyed by the historical episode concern the pressing incentives on stablecoin issuers to debase the quality of collateralization; empirical evidence on the existence of such incentives have been decisively ascertained.

Well, monetary history suggests that regulators should not wait too long to tame stablecoins, the risk being that a fast expanding market size may lead the phenomenon irreversibly out of the control of potential regulations—even baseline intuitions suggest that the size a phenomenon gauges its susceptibility to being regulated; after all, it is different to regiment a river in normal times or in a flood. In the words of Makarov and Schoar (2022), cryptocurrencies and DeFi applications can become too-big-to-regulate. For sure, current endeavors of upgrading the monetary system represent history in the making.

5.2 The Future Monetary System

"The monetary system is a crucial foundation for the economy. Every time households and businesses make payments across the range of financial transactions they place their trust in the safety of money and payment systems as a *public good*. Retaining this trust is at the core of central bank mandates" (BIS, 2022). This is how the Bank for International Settlements introduces the relevance of the monetary system. We learn from the hierarchy of money that it is the unique role of the central bank as the originator of liquidity that underlies the fundamental features of the system.

The central bank supports, directly and indirectly, the smooth functioning of payment systems. The provision of liquidity ensures that no logjams (for instance, delay in payments due to liquidity shortages of one of the parties) emerge. In addition, the central bank guarantees the finality of payments: the central bank debits the account of the ultimate payer and credits the account of the ultimate payee, so as to make payment final and irrevocable. Digital innovations must be appropriately accommodated within this architecture, not to let the disordered proliferation of new networks interact weirdly with established channels. As is often the case, the problem is how to perform the embedding, since the devil is in the details.

To begin with, one needs a clear map of the high-level objectives and properties of the monetary system, like the one in Table 1 of the BIS Report.

The first property that the Report ascribes to the future monetary system is, no wonder, **safety and stability**. Readers may have been expecting this occurrence, after the prolonged discussion of Sect. 2.2 of the monetary problem of the 2020s. This is the heritage of the crisis of 2007–2009 that has shaken the financial system at its foundations and therefore reshuffled the priorities of policymakers. In order to fit standards and deserve a place in the system, "stablecoins need to import their credibility" (lvi). This is the key aim of the forthcoming regulation of stablecoins.

The second property is **accountability**. Over the last two decades the relevance of accountability has been increasingly acknowledged in fields such as Law & Economics and Accounting Standards—one may recall a number of corporate scandals at the turn of the millennium, among which the earthshaking Enron crack. Well, the nodes of the monetary system, most prominently, banks, must be accountable and transparent to users and society. Accountability is by now a major objective of central banks as well, that has to do, among other things, with the disproportionate role that monetary policies have been playing in the advanced economies in the aftermath of the great financial crisis. Accountability can be considered part of the integrity of such institutions. One can hardly envision ways to make the objectives of DeFi align with these standards of accountability.

In this new list of priorities, **efficiency** ranks third. This may not have been the case a few decades ago when the paradigm of market efficiency was considered the cornerstone of financial thinking. Well, the great financial crisis has certified a number of destabilizing effects generated by overstretching the implications of efficiency. Think of the procyclical effects generated by marking to market the value of assets in a balance sheet. Such a practice promotes transparency and efficiency as long as markets are liquid but can result in destabilizing effects and fire sales in times of stress. The BIS (2022) envisions the efficiency of the future monetary system as essentially connected with low-cost, fast payments and throughput.

The fourth property is **inclusion**. This is one of the dimensions in which the paradigms of DeFi can stimulate institutional settings to enhance the inclusiveness of the activity. The philosophy of inclusion has received a decisive impulse in recent years, and it is natural for monetary institutions to acknowledge the properness of such instances, which not only have to do with the "justice" of arrangements but also with the economic efficiency of the system.

The BIS then considers the relevance of protecting privacy as a fundamental right and therefore promotes **user control over data**. This property marks the difference between the crypto world and the institutional system, in which trust in central authority is a basic pillar. Customers in general trust the intermediaries with which establish continuing relationship like their banks, but do not have "sufficient control" over data. New technologies may help improve such control.

The BIS further posits that the **integrity** of the system should avoid illicit activity such as fraud, money laundering or financing organized crime or terrorism. This is where the crypto system falls short of guarantees, whereas new technologies may help improve monitoring flows through the monetary system.

The seventh property of **adaptability** is considered, namely, the ability to embed technological innovations and thereby upgrade the efficiency of the system without compromising safety and stability. The monetary system should *anticipate* future developments, not let cutting-edge technologies allow the emergence of weird circuits that may endanger the stability of the overall system. The further property of **openness** concerns interoperability and flexibility, and the fact that the future system should connect a seamless network of operators, not dispersed clusters of entities.

Some readers may feel that the above properties miss the point of decentralized consensus and neglect the sophistication of the blockchain architecture. In a sense, this is true, but the point is that it *has* to be so. From a monetary perspective, the details of the technology employed in monetary arrangements (like establishing counterparty relationships or finalizing payments) are irrelevant, and in fact, should raise no questions. The information insensitivity of money is in fact a key discriminant between the kind of trust that a blockchain is meant to substitute and the trust in a money instrument (recall subsection 2.2.5 above).

From this monetary perspective, policymakers display fierce opposition to initiatives that try to evade established institutional arrangements and dismiss the above requirements.

5.2.1 From Libra to Diem

In June 2019 Facebook announced the intent to introduce the coin *Libra* as a means of payment operated by the Facebook platform, with acknowledged creators of the project being Morgan Beller, David Marcus, and Kevin Weil. Libra had been conceived as a stablecoin fully backed by cash and liquid assets and in addition, featuring a loss-absorbing capital buffer providing a further guarantee on the risk of runs. The Libra Association stated the intent not to develop its own monetary policy, but rather to inherit the monetary policy conducted on the currencies in the underlying basket.

The impact of the announcement has been remarkable. Policymakers quickly manifested with unusual emphasis a strongly negative assessment of the project. The fierce opposition of Governments, Authorities, and Central Banks seems to have caught by surprise the Libra Association. Within a few months, a number of participants in the project (among which Paypal, Visa, and Vodafone) quit the club. These entities seem to have not clearly anticipated the strategic implications of one such gigantic monetary innovation. In late 2019 the Libra Association was working on a “Libra 2.0” blueprint meant to address concerns by US regulators. The coin was rechristened *Diem* in December 2020, perhaps in order to signal that the initial negative response of central banks had been duly acknowledged in a prospective modification of the project.

An article in the Financial Times of March 10, 2022 (Murphy and Stacey 2022), reports of a breakfast featuring Fed Chair Jerome Powell and Treasury Secretary Janet Yellen on June 24, 2021, in which the conversation was about Diem. In that breakfast, the uncompromising positions expressed by Yellen seem to have aligned Powell in a rejection of Diem. The same article reports a picture of “Silicon Valley executives who thought they could charge into finance and make billions, if only they could surmount technical and regulatory barriers" (ivi).

Irrespective of the golden dreams of executives, we are in a position to acknowledge in which sense a global creator of money like Diem is something that is problematic to embed into the international monetary system. Libra/Diem was conceived to become a giant cross-border monetary aggregate practically impossible to supervise and regiment. In their opposition to the project, central banks and policymakers should not be considered to be engaged in a defense of privileges of incumbent entities, and rather to pursue the stability of the monetary system. One must recall that major threats to the stability of systems came from network effects that are ex ante difficult (to use an euphemism) to anticipate, can be overly demanding to manage ex post, and that at times result in irreversible implications; one can think for instance of the debate on the feasibility of reversing the expansionary path of the Fed's balance sheet (see Fig. 1.3). These truly concrete instances witness the relevance of the above case study.

The opposition of regulators made it clear that Diem had no future. In January 2022 the Diem Association announced the sale of its assets to Silvergate Capital Corporation.

5.3 Stablecoins

Stablecoins can be partitioned into two classes, those backed by (allegedly) safe and liquid assed, and those backed by other cryptocurrencies. The first class beckons a sort of narrow banking (i.e. one in which deposits are fully backed with reserves), to the extent that these coins are redeemable like bank deposits. Three coins, Tether, USD Coin, and Binance USS, currently dominate this class, all pegged to the US dollar. The properness of the collateralization of Tether and USD Coin has been subject to investigation and turned out to be improper. Tether has been fined $41 million by the Commodity Futures Trade Commission. Stablecoins backed by other tokens are called *algorithmic* stablecoins, and the expression programmable money is also used to denote this practice.

We are all familiar with the claim that adequate backing with safe assets (collateralization) should stabilize the price dynamics of a stablecoin pegged to an international currency. In principle, this is a sound statement. In practice, however, it is far from straightforward to design sound mechanisms for collateralization, that, recall, encompass the concrete network of *regulated* market makers supposed to hold positions in such collateral. (Advocates of stablecoins may not be paying attention enough to the relevance of the regulation of the dealers of collateral, among which custodians). In such respect, a number of cogent insights can be gleaned from the accounts of the tensions manifested by repo markets in recent years, given that collateralization schemes in repo markets work to the highest standards.

Thus, the monetary problem of stablecoins is a problem of safe assets and collateralization that has scarcely to do with the technology supporting the operation of tokens. In this sense, stablecoins are nothing new, they are simply a new form of privately produced money. However, to the extent that the public can raise questions on their backing assets, stablecoins are "not yet" money, as noticed by Gorton and Zhang (2023). The fundamental tradeoff introduced in the first page of the chapter enlightens a pivotal aspect of regulation: Gorton and Zhang argue that, currently, issuers of stablecoin seem to elect transparency as the side of the tradeoff that, at the moment, better suits their goals. This is so because stablecoins are not yet systemically regulated and therefore lack the institutional backing shared by established entities like banks. In our view, this tradeoff is the best way to enter the problem of stablecoins, which we begin to develop with a few basic questions.

5.3.1 *Basic Questions*

In an article published in the Financial Times in the aftermath of the Terra/Luna default in May 2022, Hilary Allen (2022) poses straight questions about stablecoins. The first question concerns the very existence of such coins, which claim a prominent position in the future monetary system despite the fact that they are scarcely used to pay for real-world goods and services.[3] What advantages can stablecoins claim to unfold compared with existing digital solutions that don't rely on blockchain technology? This is the first question raised by Professor Allen.

Another question concerns the inefficiency of the technology, which is in the first instance connected with limited scalability and wasteful

[3] To be fair, one must recall that not all forms of money are meant to buy goods or services. Even the best money around, base money, serves purely financial purposes in the form of bank reserves. It has been pointed out that stablecoins can add value in cross-border transactions.

use of resources to achieve decentralized consensus. One more question concerns the alleged goal of decentralization and disintermediation, being major stablecoins issued by and exchanged via centralized intermediaries like Bitfinex and Coinbase that profit from transaction fees. The resulting picture is summarized in a short sentence. "In sum, stablecoins start with a convoluted and inefficient base technology in order to avoid intermediaries, and then add intermediaries (often with apparent conflicts of interest) back in" (ivi).

Professor Allen further notices that the only truly effective way to prevent runs on stablecoins and make them truly *stable* is to put a government guarantee behind them. We shall elaborate on the regulation of stablecoins in the following chapter. Regulators are not concerned with restricting stablecoins so as to safeguard market shares of established entities like banks or digital platforms. Regulators are meant to safeguard the physiology of markets, which is a problem of safe assets and collateralization that lies at the foundations of the monetary question of the 2020s.

It matters to notice that the above critiques do not represent an a priori opposition to new digital money. Rather, these considerations build on quite established facts. Some may even consider these arguments as questioning the relevance itself of analyzing the monetary problem of stablecoins. Well, we consider it of great importance to emphasize that even if the crypto wave were to implode and evaporate within a few years, it is still worth studying and refining its description. In fact, we are currently facing a significant historical case of testing the adaptability of the monetary system to the opportunities brought about by challenging technological innovation: this is the institutional perspective of the BIS on the blockchain phenomenon, a perspective that we embrace wholeheartedly.

5.3.2 More Refined Questions

The foundational problem of safe assets and collateralization (the principle of NQA) inspires Gorton and Zhang (2023), that raise crucial questions on the nature of stablecoins, and then build a framework for devising both positive enquiries and normative approaches.

The obvious first question one may expect to hear is whether stablecoin can be considered "money" in some sense. The aforementioned tradeoff, that opens this chapter, signals that stablecoins are *not yet* money, in the sense that issuers are not yet in a position to attain states of NQA, and are currently emphasizing in their communication the properness of the collateralization adopted.

Further questions concern the nature of stablecoins in comparison with demand deposits. The extant empirical panorama represents the early days of the phenomenon, and, arguably, a primitive ecology at which to look with the prospect of a more developed system in the background. However, the concrete pattern of redemption clauses for the major stablecoins in place provides relevant empirical evidence, beginning with the notice period (the delay with which the liquidity provider fulfills the obligation of redemption) and the redemption fee. These are truly concrete gauges of the moneyness of these coins, i.e. the ability to keep their promise to pay dollars (in the form of bank money).

We learn from Gorton and Zhang (2023) that in June 2021 Tether had no notice period but featured a technical delay connected with a verification time. A variable redemption cost encompasses a withdrawal fee of 1% of the account, with the lower bound of the unit of transaction of \$1000, plus a verification fee of \$150 in Tether tokens. Other coins display even more moneyness. True USD had no notice period and up to \$30 and \$100 as domestic and international wire fees, respectively. Stably USD had no notice period and fees (however, the customer's bank may charge fees).

Redemption arrangements may well change over time, arguably, in the direction of rendering these coins more akin to standard money, and it is somewhat evident that these patterns have little to do with the specificities of the digital technology supporting the operation of coins. Well, a comprehensive look at the current panorama enables Gorton and Zhang to ascertain that stablecoins do in fact resemble demand deposits. This is an important step in the elucidation of the economic and legal (inherently intertwined) guidelines for regulating stablecoins.

To sum up, it is with the above monetary vision in the background that one can frame a logic for looking at stablecoins. Unfortunately, algorithmic stablecoins do not seem to connect with this logic, and therefore do not seem to admit a solid monetary analysis. However, "algorithmic collateralization" (an expression that may be simply nonsense) is the subject of the following case study. The rise and dramatic fall of Terra and Luna has been adequately covered by specialized media and institutional reports (see for instance BIS 2022, and the CoinDesk website). The episode is already history, and it is worth having some dates and hints at hand.

5.3.3 *Terra and Luna*

In January 2018 Do Kwon and Daniel Shin launched the project of the platform Terra as a network powering digital payment applications and stablecoins, supported by the Terra Alliance of a number of Asian e-commerce companies. In April the firm Terraform Labs that develops the blockchain is incorporated in Singapore. In April 2019 a white paper releases the details of the project. In September 2020 comes the announcement of the stablecoin TerraUSD or UST, also abbreviated Terra, meant to be pegged to the US dollar as an algorithmic stablecoin designed to adjust supply in an automated arbitrage strategy with the "companion" token Luna. In fact, the 1–1 peg of Terra to the US dollar was conceived as the promise to pay $1 worth of Luna and vice versa.

In 2021 the US Securities and Exchange Commission investigates potential violations of the laws on federal securities. Over the year Luna experienced an astonishing jump in price, moving from less than $1 to almost $90. Correspondingly, within a few months, UST has been increasing use and market capitalization, reaching $18.7 billion at its peak.

In March 2022 the crypto trader Algod bets $1 million against Do Kwon that the price of Luna will not exceed $88 a year from then. Within a few days Jump Trading, one of the investors in Luna, proposes a mechanism for deploying Bitcoin reserves in case a dramatic fall in the price of Luna would require substantial support. On April 6 the price of Luna was at its peak of almost $120 and within days UST became the third-largest stablecoin. By the end of April, the supply of Luna reached an all-time low of 346 million tokens, in order to keep up with the rising demand for UST.

In May there are signs of capital flight from UST. On May 7 Terra lost for the first time its peg to the dollar, and quotes $0.985. On May 9 Terra lost for the second time its peg. On May 11 news was broadcast that Do Kwon is one of the pseudonymous founders of the failed algorithmic stablecoin Basis Cash. On May 12 the price of Luna fell by 96%. The Terra blockchain is officially halted. On May 13 the exchanges Okx and Binance stop trading Terra tokens. At the end of May South Korean authorities displayed concerns that a hundred thousand citizens may be victims of the abrupt plunge of Terra and Luna. Magazines report of people in South Korea that sold their houses to invest in Luna, and that the crack of FTX in November 2022 had a prominent impact in this country.

It goes without saying that the Terra/Luna collapse spells doom for algorithmic stablecoins. In our view, despite the absence of proper collateralization, this short story is instructive in many senses, among which is the working of the concrete collective phenomena that accompany the fluctuations in the demand for a financial instrument. As pointed out by the BIS (2022) Report, the design of Terra/Luna contemplated incentives for investors, among which a deposit rate of 20% on UST. "As long as users had confidence in the stable value of UST and sustained market capitalization of Luna, the system could be sustained" (ivi). Well, the problem of confidence is a truly sophisticated one (as this monograph is intended to unfold), and the specific mechanism of (hopefully, proper) collateralization does not exhaust the monetary problem of stablecoins.

5.4 Central Bank Digital Currency

It is somewhat intuitive that the problem of CBDC as well is a problem of safe assets and liquidity. The fact that a central bank is in charge of the enterprise makes the problem somewhat narrowly defined, at least in comparison with stablecoins. Still, the problem is far from clear, witness the meticulous preparation of prospects and pilots that major central banks are developing. Now the problem is not the reliability of the issuer and of the instrument, but the response of the monetary system to the introduction of the instrument. In this sense, CBDC poses challenging questions that are worth studying even if the idea of a CBDC were to exit the scene within a few years. In other words, it is worth addressing the problem of CBDC *sub specie aeternitatis*, i.e. as a problem that theorists may have been conceiving decades ago before the crypto eruption.

In fact, the idea of CBDC is not a novelty of the second part of the 2010s. Back in 1992, the Bank of Finland issued the prepaid debit card Avant, that one can consider a primitive form of digital currency—the card soon turned private, and then discontinued. However, it is over the last few years that CBDC has become a structural perspective on the digital evolution of money markets. Several central banks have engaged in the design of their own CBDC, and in some cases, pilots are already at an advanced stage.

In 2017 Banco Central del Uruguay initiated a six-month pilot for the "e-peso" as an electronic platform for the national currency. Licensed service providers have been enrolled in the operation of an e-peso app allowing customers to access digital coins in exchange for paper currency. The system provided instantaneous settlement, combining anonymity with traceability. An upper bound of 30,000 e-pesos was set for individual balances, and a total of 20 million e-pesos have been issued. Importantly, bills were meant to be unique and traceable, so as to prevent double-spending. Few technical problems have manifested, and at the end of the pilot, the electronic coins have been redeemed and extinguished. The assessment of the pilot has been positive, even if no further steps seem to be expected for an e-peso.

Joint work by a set of central banks, in collaboration with the BIS, has fixed three basic principles that should underlie the issuance of CBDC. First, "do no harm": the introduction of CBDC should not interfere with the ability of the central bank to pursue objectives of price stability, financial stability, and monetary policies in general. Second, "coexistence": the introduction of CBDC should not interfere with the targeted acceptability and velocity of extant monetary aggregates. Third, "innovation and efficiency": CBDC should stand the competitive test of private digital solutions and therefore limit the eruption of private circuits whose unregulated proliferation may challenge monetary stability. These principles clearly fit the plot of the BIS (2022) for the future monetary system that we have been discussing in Sect. 5.2. Let us enter the fine-grained structure of the problem in terms of the visions of a number of central banks, that we review in strict alphabetic order.

5.4.1 *Bank of England*

In a speech at UK Finance in February 2023, Sir Jon Cunliffe—member of the BoE Financial Policy and Monetary Policy Committee and Deputy Governor for Financial Stability—unfolds the vision of the BoE on the desirability, and perhaps the necessity, to issue a digital pound within the second part of the decade. Cunliffe (BoE 2023) reviews the new panorama of innovative digital services, in particular payment services provided by non-banks, as well as the drivers that may lead to concentration in digital services (network effects, economies of scale and scope and data advantages that can act as barriers to entry). One can anticipate scenarios in which new forms of private money could drastically reduce, and possibly distort, the role of safe public money. The Speaker recalls the commitment of the BoE to continue to ensure that all types of money in the UK are interchangeable on demand to all other forms, including BoE money.

Building on these premises, Cunliffe rationalizes the potential introduction of a digital pound as a partnership with the private sector, possibly unfolding in both retail and wholesale dimensions. The BoE would provide the central infrastructure, and wallets would be operated on a "pass-through" basis, namely, wallets would hold information about ownership of balances but would pass through to the central infrastructure all of the instructions forwarded by customers. Noticeably, the technical design of the digital pound is intertwined with the forthcoming renewal of the digital infrastructure for the provision of money to commercial banks in the form of bank reserves and is also meant to connect with the new Real Time Gross Settlement system launching in 2024. There is an open attitude toward the kind of technology (possibly, of the blockchain type) that may inform the infrastructure. Programmable money is one of the themes on the table.

It has been repeatedly pointed out in the specialized media that a CBDC has the potential to displace the banking sector, and in this respect, the BoE plans restrictions on individual balances, perhaps in the range between £10,000 and £20,000. The digital pound would pay no interest. Perhaps the key point of the speech pertains to the systemic role that should be ascribed to the digital currency. The relevance of the point makes an explicit quote worth.

"In a future payments landscape, there could be opportunities for privately issued stablecoins, regulated to the same standards as we regulate other forms of privately issued money. We envisage that these could operate alongside commercial bank money and cash. The digital pound could act as a bridging asset between different types of privately issued digital money and establish standards for interoperability. And, crucially, the requirement for privately issued digital money to be exchangeable on demand and at par for Bank of England digital pounds would help secure the interchangeability and uniformity of money in the UK." At stake, then, is not only the liquidity backstop for (properly regulated) stablecoin issuers, but more generally the physiology of the monetary system.

This quote provides one more justification for our crude sketch of Chapter 2 of the monetary problem of the 2020s. In the absence of adequate perspective, the content of the above quote may be interpreted as simply targeting standards of best practice and functioning, i.e. problems of efficiency. However, there is much more than efficiency at stake in the quote. At stake is the ordered well functioning and the physiology itself of the system, which does not admit a disordered growth of short circuits and superposition with extant arrangements. Cunliffe himself notices that the role of "bridging assets" concerns ensuring convertibility between different platforms. This is about the concrete market structure, namely, the concrete network of (digital) market makers at play.

The key point is that, in times of stress, agents, and entities try to adjust positions, and collective flights to safety typically result in bottlenecks and market squeezes. Again, the disordered growth of the shadow banking system at the turn of the millennium is a cogent example of the necessity to keep the *entire* system in control once new circuits are expected to enter the arena. The role of "bridging asset" ascribed to the digital currency would be an *endogenous* property, much as a highway is simply a possible route, and it is the endogenous amount of drivers willing to use the infrastructure that shapes the endogenous properties of the traffic dynamics. In such respect, restrictions on individual balances may place inherent limits on these endogenous effects.

No decision as yet has been taken by the BoE concerning the effective introduction of a digital pound, and the next (from 2023) three years shall be devoted to the development of a thorough study (encompassing a technical blueprint) that will make the BoE in a position to assess properly the desirability of exercising the option of effectively issuing the digital pound. "We expect that this research and development work will have important benefits for both the Bank and the fintech industry even if the eventual decision is not to introduce a digital pound" (ivi).

The speech by Cunliffe represents a nice introduction to the broad theme of CBDC, in that the views of the BoE are largely representative of those of other big players like the Fed or the ECB. In particular, Cunliffe makes it clear in which sense a digital pound is a policy option conceived as part of a *complete contingent plan* concerning the smooth embedding of new digital functions and tokens into the UK monetary system. Analogous priorities are documented by the European Central Bank.

5.4.2 *European Central Bank*

The ECB has publicly stated the timeline of the project of the digital euro, conceived as a form of central bank money accessible to all citizens and firms. In the third quarter of 2023, a decision-making document is expected to sharpen the details of the project, whose key elements are discussed in the Report on a digital euro (ECB 2020) as an instrument supposed to complement notes in circulation and commercial bank money, with specific reference to retail offline payments. The prospective digital euro, which must be consistent with the mandate of the ECB, is subject to a scenario analysis providing the logic of the project. Seven scenarios are considered.

The first scenario concerns the innovative digital endeavors that are reshaping the potentiality of money markets. In such respects, the introduction of a digital euro may foster the digitalization of the economy. Among other things, a digital euro could facilitate the development of supervised intermediaries providing end-user solutions accessible to consumers, encompassing the distribution of both commercial bank money and central bank money. The architecture of the system should be flexible, so as to allow easy integration of new types of devices over time.

A second scenario concerns the well-established secular decline in the relative use of cash with respect to digital payments, that, beyond a certain point, could endanger the sustainability of the physical cash infrastructure.[4] In this respect, a digital euro may represent an additional form of public money and means of payment, that should be cheap to use, secure, safe, efficient, and easy to use even for unskilled individuals. In this sense, the properties of the digital euro should resemble those of physical cash.

A third scenario concerns the competitiveness of a digital euro as a credible alternative to central bank money, commercial bank deposits, and digital money, an alternative that can help avoid the drawbacks of the diffusion of instruments (like stablecoins) not denominated in euro. These phenomena may weaken, or even impair, the transmission of monetary policy in the euro area, and in fact, threaten political sovereignty.

[4] This is the scenario occurring in Sweden. It is worth recalling the commitment of the Eurosystem to guarantee freedom of choice in payment: the Eurosystem is in charge of ensuring access to physical cash for all citizens.

A fourth scenario concerns the potentially manifesting desirability of a digital euro as an instrument for the transmission of monetary policy. The central bank may use the remuneration of the digital euro as a policy lever meant to influence direct consumption and investment choices (This is a line of departure between the views of ECB and BoE, which does not ascribe a monetary policy role to the would-be digital pound).

A fifth scenario concerns potential shocks that may (perhaps temporarily) endanger the well-functioning of private payment systems, for instance, cyber incidents, natural disasters, and other extreme events. Under these contingencies, a digital euro, together with physical cash, would help stabilize the functioning of payments in the absence of private solutions.

A sixth scenario concerns the international role of the euro, which may suffer from the issuance of CBDC by other major central banks. The ECB envisions the benefits of a cooperative approach to interoperable designs of CBDCs across currencies, which may help correct inefficiencies in existing cross-currency payment infrastructures. A seventh scenario concerns the potential role of a digital euro as a catalyst of innovation in manifold dimensions, among which ecological prospects. The above scenario analysis confirms that central banks are focusing on the role of a CBDC as part of a complete contingent plan, namely, as an option that may be exercised, once a proper design of the infrastructure is ultimately fixed.

As expected, the ECB Report discusses potential drawbacks concerning a digital euro that may displace banking activities. The introduction of a digital euro may induce investors to transform their commercial bank deposits into central bank liabilities. Among the effects of this dynamics, banks might have to deleverage and decrease the supply of credit, thus altering the investment process in the real economy. Definitely, this is among the major criticalities of the CBDC construct. Further issues pertain to whether the digital euro should be accessible directly to households and firms, or indirectly via intermediaries.

Recent official statements emphasize that a digital euro will never be programmable money. This is another point at which the vision of the ECB differentiates from that of the BoE.

5.4.3 *Sveriges Riksbank*

Sweden is an interesting case study that differentiates from the pair above. The attitude of the BoE compares with that of the ECB in looking at CBDC as an option that is worth considering, despite the fact that the "exercise value" of the option—the feasibility and desirability of a CBDC on both social and monetary grounds—may be hard to estimate even qualitatively. The attitude of the Sveriges Riksbank (SR) toward the CBDC construct is intertwined with the marginal and continuously shrinking role of physical cash in the country.

For a number of reasons, Sweden has been for decades experiencing a fast decline in the use of physical cash. One for sure acknowledges the availability of technological solutions and the preferences of customers; however, diseconomies of scale of running a network of distribution of physical cash in that country can be considered among the idiosyncrasies of the Swedish case. Columnists around the world further argue about the desirability of eliminating physical cash to further compress criminal activity in Sweden—perhaps displaying a naïve assessment of the potential of criminal minds. For sure, the krona does not share the market size and systemic role of currencies like the euro or the UK sterling, and the attitude of Swedish authorities toward CBDC is to a large extent focused on issues of efficiency, in both technical and economic dimensions. In this sense, Sweden can be considered an "extreme" case study for the development of a CBDC.

Needless to say, the national banking system has displayed serious concerns about the potential of an e-krona to displace banking activities. In response, Swedish authorities have been actively paying attention to this problem and decisively emphasized the features of the project that pertain to the two-tier structure of the architecture that gives banks a key role. Communications of the SR (see SR 2023) provide clear accounts of the already advanced state of the e-krona project.

A newly built offline digital infrastructure that parallels the private payment system is the environment of the e-krona, which targets a two-tier setup. Corda is the name of the DLT platform on which the e-krona pilot is built. A fundamental aspect of the project is that the e-krona is meant to provide a backstop for private payment circuits. Here one notices some analogy with the would-be digital pound as a "bridging asset" envisioned by Jon Cunliffe. On more technical grounds, one notices that the e-krona is a register-based coin, rather than a value-based correspondent. Programmability is one of the points emphasized by the SR as relevant for the potential of the e-krona to unfold. This is an instance of technical efficiency.

Economic efficiency as well is targeted by the SR. For instance, the complete range of possible levels of governance in the digital network is currently scrutinized. A low level of governance may enable private entities to exploit their potential for designing innovative services, thereby promoting competition and innovation, but may at the same time make it difficult for the public to have a sharp appreciation of the nature of digital money. At the other extreme, a high level of governance would ensure uniformity in the supply of services for the digital coin, thereby inhibiting competition and innovation. How to strike a balance between such extremes is an ongoing reflection.

In the current phase 3 of the pilot, the e-krona joins the "Icebreaker" cooperation project with the Bank of Israel, Norges Bank and the BIS for testing the efficiency of cross-border payments. The project develops a model for different networks to communicate via a hub that enables payment messages to be sent between the individual CBDC networks; cross-currency payments are executed using FX providers that participate in at least a pair of CBDC networks.

Currently, no decision on the issuance of an e-krona has been stated, nor on how digital money could be designed or what technology might be used.

5.4.4 Uncharted Territory

The above accounts of the visions of different central banks on CBDC display clearly the complexity of the problem at hand. Columnists are engaged in building their own perspectives on the problem.

On the one hand, advocates of the merits of CBDC enroll a list of beneficial effects on the financial environment. They envision the financial system as somehow incomplete with respect to recent digital innovations, and the CBDC as a means to complete the money market, in both retail and wholesale dimensions. On the other hand, skeptics point out that the enterprise seems to be driven essentially by technological targets, as part of a complete contingency plan whose consequences, however, may be hard to keep under control. In all probability, the impact on the international monetary system of CBDCs will be, to some extent, a game changer.

It has been pointed out that CBDC may embody the potential to promote financial inclusion and innovation. However, as is often the case, financial innovation comes at the cost of risks that are far from straightforward to anticipate. A key problem is to harmonize the CBDC construct with the hierarchy of money, that is, a problem of market design. Access to CBDC—either retail or wholesale—by citizens and firms arguably introduces layers of token exchange not in line with the hierarchy of account-based money and flowing through circuits with partially unclear counterparty risk patterns. It is for this reason that pilot experiments are delicately entering uncharted territory. In this respect, China stands out.

In 2014 the People's Bank of China (PBC) started research on the feasibility of a national currency. In 2017 the research group was established as the Digital Currency Research Institute. The prime focus of the project concerned digital payments, with the aim of improving retail payments, interbank clearing, and cross-border payments. In 2018 a paper by Yao Qian released the details of the project. In particular, three centers for identification, registration, and big-data analysis are identified. Coins are stored in digital wallets operated by financial intermediaries. The PBC provides payment clearing and settlement infrastructure as the first layer of the two tier system. The second layer is operated by chartered financial institutions, so as to let Telecom operators and other online payment platforms access the system.

News (see He 2023) report increasing commitment of Chinese authorities in the preparation of the national rollout of the e-CNY. In January 2023 the PBC released a wallet app for Apple and Android that can be used in the regions involved in the pilot. Monetary incentives have also been set in place. "Several Chinese cities, including Beijing and Shenzhen, have even given away millions of dollars in digital yuan to their residents outright, encouraging them to use the virtual money" (ivi).

China is currently among the countries with a more advanced state of progress of CBDC experimenting, and perhaps the country that has taken the more decisive steps in the exploration of the uncharted territory uncovered by a CBDC. Concrete use of the e-CNY already occurs as legal tender, and businesses accepting digital payments like Alipay are now required to accept the sovereign digital coin. However, the Chinese experience seems to raise scarce enthusiasm in Western economies.

A number of columnists have stated explicitly that central banks should beware of the lure of CBDC. There are serious concerns, for instance concerning monetary policy. In a meeting at the House of Lords

Economic Affairs Committee, a BoE governor has been stressing the point that CBDC is not about monetary policy. The committee chair replied: "But it could be." The idea of CBDC has even been met with derision (see Muir 2023). In the words of Prasad (2021), central banks run the gauntlet. In our view, this backlash should not be considered to diminish the relevance of exploring the general properties of the CBDC construct. The world is going digital in manifold directions, and money is one such dimension.

The content of this section may inspire the analysis of regulation that we undertake in the following chapter. Laws and regulations, in general and whatever the phenomena under consideration, are meant to regiment idiosyncrasies and prevent and prosecute dishonest behavior and crime, so as to achieve *standards* of appropriate social interaction; in this attempt, legislators and regulators typically implement the dictates of general principles. Well, this is exactly what central banks are pursuing, albeit in a highly specific setting, with the introduction of CBDC.

References

Allen H. (2022). We're asking the wrong questions about stablecoins. Financial Times, May 25.

BIS (Bank for International Settlements, 2022). The future monetary system. Annual Economic Report.

Board of Governors of the Federal Reserve System (2022). Money and payments: the U.S. dollar in the age of digital transformation. January.

BoE (Bank of England, 2023). The digital pound—speech by Jon Cunliffe.

ECB (European Central Bank, 2020). Report on a digital euro. October.

Gintis H. (2009). The Bounds of Reason. Princeton University Press.

Gorton G. B., Zhang J. Y. (2023). Taming wildcat stablecoins. University of Chicago Law Review 90 (3), 909–971.

He L. (2023). China makes major push in its ambitious digital yuan project. CNN, April 24.

Makarov I., Schoar A. (2022). Cryptocurrencies and Decentralized Finance. BIS Working Paper No 1061.

Muir M. (2023). Central banks' digital currency plans face public backlash. Financial Times, March 13.

Murphy H., Stacey K. (2022). Facebook Libra: the inside story of how the company's cryptocurrency dream died. Financial Times, March 10.
North D. C. (1991). Institutions. Journal of Economic Perspectives 5 (1), 97–112.
Prasad E. S. (2021). The Future of Money. Harvard University Press.
SR (Sveriges Riksbank, 2023). E-krona pilot, phase 3. April.

CHAPTER 6

Regulation

Abstract This chapter summarizes the major principles for the regulation of new digital coins that feature in the current debate. Again, the principle of "no questions asked" represents the logical cornerstone of the theme. It is emphasized that officials can take action against (and in fact have prosecuted) misconduct even in the absence of specific regulation of new instruments. Following Gorton and Zhang, the proper regulation of stablecoins is argued to resemble that of banks as depository institutions. In such respect, the theoretical problem of what is a bank is discussed as far from settled. Among the key issues, one acknowledges the synergy between the sides of the balance sheet and the special liquidity backstops available.

Keywords Regulation · Stablecoin · Bank · Demand Deposit Liability · Narrow Banking

The great financial crisis of 2007–2009 has provoked impressive regulatory responses that have been severely questioned. For instance, the Dodd–Frank Act, signed into law by Barack Obama in 2010, has been criticized, among other things, for its monstrous size, and for the high

A. Schianchi and A. Mantovi, *The Economics of Cryptocurrencies and Digital Money*, Palgrave Studies in Financial Services Technology,
https://doi.org/10.1007/978-3-031-44248-3_6

compliance costs. It has been conjectured that this gigantic regulatory wave may have somewhat inhibited the regulatory response to the crypto eruption. Still, the debate on the regulation of new digital tokens is intense and proposals abound, among which regulating crypto as gambling. A comprehensive overview of the debate is beyond our goals, and in this brief chapter we shall concentrate on the basic criticalities at stake. Even within these limits, however, we will find it mandatory to step back to the foundations of banking and to emphasize the desirability of harmonizing regulatory frameworks.

There is a fundamental hiatus between the normative problems of businesses and societies. A private business has typically sharp objectives, among which profit maximization and shareholder value maximization stand on top of the list, perhaps accompanied by market share and technological targets. Societies (represented by regulators) have more nuanced economic objectives, and regulators are forced to pursue a (not always sharply defined) list of objectives of, say, aggregate and redistributive welfare, stability, and appropriate risk allocation. There is an inherent hiatus between these two perspectives; still, the normative problem of the private business of banking is part and parcel of the debate on the regulation of socially valuable money markets, as this chapter unfolds. Recall, it is one of the basic results of Diamond and Dybvig (1983) that bank runs can damage the entire economy; this is a fundamental truth that, noticeably, is called into question every time governments are required to rescue financial entities in trouble.

Following the lines of argument that we have been unfolding in previous chapters, we envision the principle of NQA as the cornerstone of monetary regulation. Let us start by reminding ourselves that it has been the deposit insurance regulation (introduced in the US in 1933) that ended the era of bank runs: insurance guarantees no questions asked. The regulation of new tokens should pursue the same prime aim. However, much regulation is already in place, and it is stimulating to begin the chapter with a case study.

6.1 A Case Study

In recent years US officials have been active in prosecuting misconduct in the crypto arena. The Office of the General Attorney of New York has been conducting investigations into the operations of Bitfinex and Tether. Bitfinex is a trading platform that allows customers to deposit currency, buy virtual currencies, and convert them back into standard currency. Tether, we all know, is among the superstars of stablecoins, and is pegged 1–1 to the US dollar. Both constructs are operations of subsidiaries of Hong Kong-based iFinex. Investigations ascertained misconduct.

From its inception in 2014, Tether has been declared to be fully backed by US dollars. This lasted until February 2019, when statements were changed to being fully backed by reserves encompassing cash equivalents and other claims. For several months in 2017, Tether was not backed by a significant bank relationship, and could not process direct fiat deposits for purchases of tokens by customers. Investigations ascertained that Tether did not inform clients and markets that, from June 1 to September 15, coins were not backed 1–1 by proper reserves.

Investigations further enlightened the details of the relationship of Bitfinex with Crypto Capital Corp. By mid-2018, Crypto Capital held over $1 billion in funds from Bitfinex clients. A freeze of funds of Crypto Capital resulted in an internal liquidity crisis, but Bitfinex continued to direct clients to utilize Crypto Capital. Online reports documented the inability or unwillingness of Bitfinex to timely process client withdrawal requests. Investigations ascertained further problems with lack of proper backing of the coin and misrepresentation to clients.

In April 2019 the prosecution entered the Supreme Court in New York. Arrangements resulted in the Office of the General Attorney accepting a settlement agreement in lieu of commencing a statutory proceeding for violation of the Martin Act and Executive Law. Respondents agreed to pay $18.5 million (the "Monetary Relief Amount") for closing the dispute, promising transparent disclosures about collateralization from there on. Bitfinex and Tether are no longer allowed to perform trading activity in New York; they are allowed to provide services like blockchain analysis or risk-scoring.

Among the instructive insights conveyed by the case study one notices that the Office of the Attorney General has been conducting investigations pursuant to the Martin Act introduced exactly a century ago, when cryptocurrencies were not in the dreams of even the more creative fellows. General Attorney Letitia James and collaborators have shown that it does not necessarily take new regulation to address new phenomena—in this respect, the system of Common Law displays decisive advantages with respect to Civil Law. Among other things, *enforcing* new regulations can be a truly sophisticated task.

6.2 Basic Ideas

The need to regulate Bitcoin (and the like) has been largely acknowledged in the early days of the phenomenon, among the reasons being the illegal activities that seem to use the platform as a vehicle. The recent crypto downfall has provided further elements for the elucidation of matters of principle. Economists typically acknowledge the significant insights provided by empirical evidences of instabilities.

In a comment to the recent crypto downfall, The Economist argues that regulators should be guided by two principles. "One is to ensure that theft and fraud are minimised, as with any financial activity. The other is to keep the mainstream financial system insulated from further crypto-ructions." It is further argued that crypto exchanges should be required to back customer deposits with liquid assets, and to comply with standards of disclosure on the properness of collateralization. We do align wholeheartedly with such remarks, that, after all, represent plain good sense. On top of that, one acknowledges the fundamental problem of making the public aware of the riskiness of the phenomenon.

Institutions and media are actively engaged in this task, which, as already pointed out, is among the goals of our work. Much like Bitcoin miners are self-appointed and aware of the costs and expected revenues, so crypto investors should self-select themselves as well aware of the nature of the crypto ecology. Gemini is one of the entities involved in the crypto downfall of 2022. Investors in Gemini were confident of having access to deposits as secure as banks. It turned out not to be so, irrespective of what good intentions of the management of Gemini had been.

In the previous chapter, we have been arguing that an advanced institutional setting is not compatible with the kind of "anonymity" of actors that relates to evading authentication of identity, and therefore prosecutability. Along similar lines, Makarov and Schoar (2022) envision the key challenges of the regulation of cryptocurrencies as connected with the pseudonymous and jurisdiction-free nature of the phenomenon. Permissionless protocols and smart contracts have the potential to remove the boundaries between the financial systems of different countries, and open channels of regulatory arbitrage that regulators aim to prevent. According to the Authors, regulation at the level of developers and validators can represent a crucial step for further developments, concerning in the first instance verification of identity and certification that crypto addresses belong to confirmed users. Not only we do align with such a vision, but we seem to notice some insightful connections with the theoretical problem of the TSS that we have been sketching in Sect. 2.2.

Taking an extreme position, one may even argue that cryptocurrencies have been conceived as a means of exchange, and that regulators should ban their exchange as an asset class. However, much talk has been devoted to the benefits of decentralized finance, among which financial inclusion, so that a drastically stringent regulation may be considered a hindrance to the potential benefits of crypto, that many believe should be allowed to unfold to some extent. Keeping in mind that the crypto sector "suffers from inherent shortcomings in stability, efficiency, accountability and integrity that can only be partially addressed by regulation. [...] Importantly, these flaws derive from the underlying economics of incentives, not from technological constraints. And, no less significantly, these flaws would persist even if regulation and oversight were to address the financial instability problems and risk of loss implicit in crypto" (BIS 2022). It is somewhat natural to advocate that the crypto ecology should be grounded on the secure foundations provided by central banks.

To a large extent, the above considerations hold for stablecoins as well. True, we can be more precise on the regulation of stablecoins.

6.3 Stablecoins as Privately Produced Money

Stablecoins are meant to behave as money. In fact, as long as they are accepted as means of exchange and redeemable at par with a standard currency, they behave like money. The caveat is *as long as*. The principle of NQA is at stake: a stablecoin behaves as money as long as NQA holds. It is this simple. However, the economic problem is profound.

Recent turbulence has shown that stablecoins have largely failed on their promise, with the Terra-Luna crack as a staggering empirical rejection of stability. Admittedly, the algorithmic nature of the coins involved may be considered crucial in the fatal event, and some may argue that proper collateralization (that should represent the norm of stablecoins) may have changed things a lot. For sure it is worth emphasizing the lack of a complete contingent plan in case of runs. This, in our view, should be an essential part of the regulation of stablecoins, at least as relevant as the problem of collateralization.

All in all, stablecoins have displayed instabilities that had not been expected, and the point is how to fix the problem in general terms. Well, it has become clearer over the last decade in which sense it is the network of liquidity backstops that pivot the stability of the hierarchy of money. In the simplest example, deposit insurance stems runs; in more recent representations, the liquidity facilities run by central banks are there to stem panics generated by liquidity shortages.

The problem is given a historical perspective by Gorton and Zhang (2023). The "free banking" era in the US is a paradigmatic episode manifesting the problems generated by privately produced money. Starting with 1837, a number of States allowed chartered banks to issue their own banknotes. Such banknotes were in principle meant to represent the same unit of value (the "dollar"), but were in practice exchanged at (varying) discounts that gauged the (varying) perceived riskiness of the issuer bank, or, equivalently, the distance from the perfect trustworthiness targeted by the NQA principle. Truly sharp insights then emerged from the advent of the MMMF, again in the US, in the late 1970s.

The phenomenon can be interpreted as a regulatory arbitrage. The Glass-Steagall Act (of 37 pages!) introduced in 1933 prohibited paying interests on demand deposits, and mandated a cap on interests on term deposits, with the Federal Reserve in charge of setting the cap periodically. This "Regulation Q" (that has been in place until 2011) has not been binding for decades since the cap was set well above market rates. Then came the 1970s and the double-digit inflation that features in macroeconomic manuals. The demand for higher yield stimulated a regulatory arbitrage, and the MMMF emerged as an entity issuing deposit-like liabilities paying interests above the legal cap. The asset side of the entity, evidently, had to be properly conceived in order to achieve substantial liquidity.

The case was raised whether this should be considered a violation of regulation Q: in primis, it had to be established whether the MMMF had to be considered within the perimeter of the regulation. The debate then developed as a query of whether MMMFs should be considered issuing equity or debt. Regulators argued that owners of MMMF shares were holding shares of *ownership*, thereby establishing that the MMMF was outside the perimeter of regulation Q, with the implication of nonexistence of conflict with the same regulation. On the contrary, Gorton and Zhang (2023) argue that it was obvious that the economic content of a MMMF share was equivalent to a demand deposit, and that it was the economic incentives that should have informed the interpretation of MMMF shares, not the legal status.

The above remarks establish a fundamental lesson. New tokens like stablecoins call for a proper monetary representation in order to fit the existing regulatory framework in a sound way. Stablecoins aim at substituting other means of exchange and stores of value. As such, they must be made to fit the monetary regulation that applies to the instruments that they aim to substitute, and regulators should avoid pursuing multiple special charters and rather aim at a uniform regulatory framework. Gorton and Zhang (2023) envision a pair of possibilities for building a regulatory setup in the US.

First, the Financial Stability Oversight Council could designate stablecoin issuance as a systemic payment system under Title VIII of the Dodd–Frank Act, thereby fixing a scene in which definite standards should be fixed by the Federal Reserve for clearing and supervision. The Federal Reserve could then require stablecoins to be issued from FDIC-insured banks or require 1–1 backing with reserves. As a second possibility, the Congress can pass new legislation that promotes stablecoins as public money, for instance by requiring stablecoin issuers to become FDIC-insured banks subject to regulation and supervision as other banks. Clearly, both proposals aim at uniformity in the legal framework.

To sum up. "Stablecoins will not be the last attempt to create private money with new technology. But the fundamental economic concepts remain identical—namely, if an entity is offering a business that is essentially equivalent to taking deposits, then regulate that entity as a bank and require it to obtain deposit insurance" (ivi).

One may have been arguing at the outset, a priori, that stablecoins should be regulated as demand deposits, as a matter of plain good sense. It takes much more than good sense, though, to tailor explicit regulations, and design effective enforcement and monitoring—witness the recent default of the Silicon Valley Bank. Among other things, it takes a detailed understanding of the banking business. Unfortunately, there is no decentralized consensus on what the banking business should be, and we find it proper to sketch at least the turning points of the debate. The following paragraph, evidently, makes no justice of the theoretical problem of banking, and still may help improve one's view on why and how stablecoins should be made to fit the map of banking regulation.

6.4 What is a Bank

On positive grounds, there is little doubt that banks run leverage ratios much larger than nonfinancial companies and that short-term debt is a key element of their capital structure. Banks are largely financed by deposits and are in fact in the business of creating money out of their assets. Still, the normative debate on the nature of banks is far from settled. This may sound puzzling, given the number of economists and regulators that have been tackling the problem since, say, the financial panic initiated in 1929, and in more recent years have been more or less directly involved in the design of Basel regulations. To date, there is no universally accepted model of the "physiology" of banking.

There exist of course authoritative treatises that cover the economics of banking and the financial instruments that shape the architecture of risk management—concerning interest rate risk, market risk, credit risk, and operational risk—as driver of the allocation of resources and creation of value. These complementary perspectives provide a comprehensive overview of the operations of banks (and, to a large extent, or intermediaries in general) and of what regulations should be concerned with, in first instance constraints on balance sheet variables like equity ratios and leverage ratios, and liquidity requirements. However, there seem to persist unresolved tensions between the logic that inspires economists and regulators. In fact, even among economists one finds conflicting views on what banks should do, and, remarkably, on the map itself of the theoretical landscape.

For a long time, the microeconomics of banking has been a slippery terrain, there being no role for banks in a frictionless perfectly competitive scenario in which securities and deposits are perfect substitutes (see Freixas and Rochet 2008). The breakthroughs of information economics in the 1970s have drastically altered the scene; asymmetric information and the screening activity of banks have been assumed as pivotal issues for rationalizing the emergence of banks from a preliminary Modigliani–Miller (MM) scene. In recent years, the renewed problem of liquidity (see Tirole 2011) has definitely enriched the structure of the inquiry, taking on board fundamental insights by Hyman Minsky (1986) on the management of cash inflows and outflows, as well as progresses in the understanding of the interplay of market liquidity and funding liquidity (see for instance Krishnamurthy 2010; de Bandt et al. 2021). The essence of banking as *spread* (return on assets minus cost of capital) business and the criticality of maturity mismatch have been thereby refocused, in search of the natural coordinates of the theoretical landscape, and of the natural ecology of banks.

It is somewhat intuitive that banks have no role in a frictionless MM world where I can buy myself a beer with a slice of my wealth stock. Perfect liquidity is guaranteed in the MM world, and no entity can profit from the production of liquid claims. It is less intuitive to draw the essential role of liquidity in a more realistic world, in which the demand for liquid claims can be represented either as exogenous or endogenous. DeAngelo and Stulz (2015) take the former stance.

The Authors tailor a stylized model of banking as the production of liquid claims that have a social value. The model features an exogenously given demand for liquid claims, that manifests itself as a liquidity premium. The Authors further posit that banks have an advantage in circumventing frictions that other intermediaries are not well equipped to address. The empirical soundness of this assumption rests of course on the privileged position of actual commercial banks in the hierarchy of money—they have direct access to the central bank balance sheet and privileged access to a number of facilities, most notably amid a turbulence[1]; furthermore, they typically originate the tree of counterparties that shape financial markets. The aforementioned advantage allows banks to make profits by arbitraging different capital markets and producing liquid claims on an economically sound basis. Crucial in such respects is the ability of banks to engage in risk management and hedging practices that render *safe* and liquid the asset side of the balance sheet.

In the model, the monetary function of banks is "stripped-to-the-basics" as a means to strike a position in the debate on the normative essence of banking. The model implies that it is optimal for banks to maximize leverage. This conclusion represents a stylized instance of the relevance of debt financing[2] for banks, something on which economists and regulators typically agree (see for instance Aiyar et al. 2015). The logic of taking to the limit the relevance of debt financing is meant to challenge the idea of equity-financed banking that has regained

[1] At the time of writing we are witnessing the Federal Reserve actively engaged in supporting the US banks that have suffered from the crack of the Silicon Valley Bank.

[2] The model is too stylized to stage the disciplinary role of debt, that represents a cornerstone of corporate finance. A generalization of the model may do the job.

momentum in the 2010s in the discussion on how to make banks intrinsically safe. A bank 100% equity-financed has no short-term debt capital prone to runs, and the equity capital can absorb temporary losses on the asset side. One can hardly question the inspiration of the equity-financed construct, and still challenge the economic soundness of the design, that marks a decisive departure from actual standards.

The legal status of banks in Italy is fixed in the Testo Unico Bancario as entities entitled (chartered) to engage in both deposit taking and lending. In addition, banks are actively engaged in the operation of payment systems, and in particular the large value payment system governed by the correspondent central bank (Target2 in the eurozone). This picture holds somewhat uniformly across borders and continents. The two activities of lending and deposit taking are in principle independent of one another, and it has been argued that the pairing is more a historical legacy than a physiology. However, a number of Authors have depicted instances of one such physiology. For instance, the model discussed by Kashiap et al. (2002) emphasizes the synergy between the two activities when the oscillations in the demand for redemption by depositors are not positively correlated with takedowns on loan commitments.

The model is quite general in representing banks as producers of liquidity on both sides of the balance sheet and is quite sharp in making explicit why liquidity emerges as the pivotal dynamics that is at the same time the *synergy and the criticality* of the pairing of the basic activities on the two sides of the balance sheet. There is a large consensus on the theoretical soundness of such arguments; still, whether or not this should be considered the physiology of banking is a matter of controversy.

In the wake of the great financial crisis of 2007–2009, advocates of the separation of banking activities have been renewing arguments about the desirability of narrow banking and equity-financed banking. Narrow banking poses constraints on the asset side of the balance sheet (100% reserves) so as to fix the problems of fractional reserve. For our purposes, it is more interesting to focus the constraints on the liability side of the balance sheet, which stages the monetary function of banks, and follow Andolfatto (2016a, 2016b) in challenging the "dream" of equity-financed banking.

Banks produce liquidity on the RHS of the balance sheet by issuing demand deposit liabilities; people want such claims to have a nominal anchor, namely, to trade at par with certainty with central bank money on demand. Equity financing can hardly support the fixed exchange rate of par between base money and bank money. The monetary function of banks is blurred in the equity-financed scheme; other entities would be required to enter the scene and create bank money, that represents a fundamental monetary aggregate in the contemporary financial ecology. And here we return to the hierarchy of money; you can hardly reshape the hierarchy by separating banking activities without an overall reshuffling of the monetary flows in the system. Not to talk about the strategic games of counterparties.

From our game theoretic standpoint, it is worth noticing that the landmark article by Diamond and Dybvig (1983) remains the guiding light for appreciating the strategic delicacy of liquidity production. The model game therein provides an explicit analytic setting for envisioning the principle of NQA at play. Bank runs are inherently strategic phenomena, and guarantees (backstops) shift the equilibrium of the game from run to safety (on account of trust in the effectiveness of the guarantee). There exists decentralized consensus on the foundational status of the picture of Diamond and Dybvig (1983), that applies also to the recent crypto downfall.

At this point we seem to have depicted the pivotal questions of the debate on banking. With no ambition to assess the "right" nature of banking, we can state that, once the monetary function of banks is at stake, the above models address the pivotal criticalities at play, that are not in dispute and that characterize stablecoins as well in their ambition of being money. Somewhat more controversial may be striking a position with respect to the ideal MM framework as the proper benchmark scenario for the analysis of banking, i.e. as the natural stage for the introduction of whatever set of frictions one may be interested in. Let us simply notice that one can advocate a different position.

In our view, the stylized picture set forth by DeAngelo and Stulz (2015) provides a truly cogent and useful starting scenario, that, among other things, is quite natural to embed into the hierarchy of money. The fundamental frictions and the baseline business model fix a sound analytical platform for adding further aspects of the normative picture of banking. After all, starting with the MM framework, one must then justify the emergence of banks by introducing suitable frictions, eventually rediscovering (something close to) the picture of DeAngelo and Stulz (2015). There is a sort of discontinuity at play: in the frictionless MM limit, banks need not exist (something more profound than the irrelevance of the capital structure); then, when a minimal set of frictions happens to justify the existence of stylized banking, all of a sudden, the optimal capital structure of banks is well defined (maximize debt). To develop a detailed representation of the smooth transition between the two benchmark scenes would represent a truly instructive chapter of the theory of banking. For sure, in a map of the possible frictions at play, the perfect MM world is somewhat distant from the actual ecology of banks.

With that said, one such theoretical stance in no way influences our conclusions on the regulation of stablecoins. One may well consider the MM framework as a sound benchmark of analysis and find no contradiction with the discussion by Gorton and Zhang (2023). True, the picture of DeAngelo and Stulz (2015) is more insightful, being an explicit business model from which issuers of stablecoins should not depart drastically, and to some extent, intermediaries and investors in crypto as well. We have already pointed out the unsound balance sheet of Alameda, whose LHS consisted largely of tokens created by FTX.

To sum up, this brief chapter was meant to deepen the senses in which the regulation of stablecoins should compare with the regulation of banks as issuers of demand deposit liabilities. This may be scarcely surprising but is a truly relevant point in the logical separation between, on the one hand, the innovative technological aspects of the recent wave of digital tokens, and, on the other hand, the inherently associated monetary problems, that remain the same.

References

Aiyar S., Calorimis C. W., Weladek T. (2015). Bank capital regulation: theory, empirics, and policy. IMF Economic Review 63 (4), 955–983.

Andolfatto D. (2016a). On Cochrane's dream of equity-financing banking. Macromania blog, May 2.

Andolfatto D. (2016b). Some questions concerning equity-financed banking. Macromania blog, May 29.

de Bandt O., Lecarpentier S., Pouvelle C. (2021). Determinants of banks' liquidity: a French perspective on interactions between market and regulatory requirements. Journal of Banking and Finance 124, 1–18.

BIS (Bank for International Settlements, 2022). The future monetary system. Annual Economic Report.

DeAngelo H., Stulz, R. M. (2015). Liquid-claim production, risk management, and bank capital structure: why high leverage is optimal for banks. Journal of Financial Economics 116, 219–236.

Diamond D., Dybvig P. H. (1983). Bank runs, deposit insurance, and liquidity. Journal of Political Economy 91 (3), 401–419.
Freixas X., Rochet J. C. (2008). Microeconomics of Banking. Second edition. The MIT Press.
Gorton G. B., Zhang J. Y. (2023). Taming wildcat stablecoins. University of Chicago Law Review 90 (3), 909–971.
Kashiap A. K., Rajan R., Stein J. C. (2002). Banks as liquidity providers: an explanation for the coexistence of lending and deposit-taking. Journal of Finance 57 (1), 33–73.
Krishnamurthy A. (2010). Amplification mechanisms in liquidity crises. American Economic Journal: Macroeconomics 2, 1–30.
Makarov I., Schoar A. (2022). Cryptocurrencies and Decentralized Finance. BIS Working Paper No 1061.
Minsky H. (1986). Stabilizing an Unstable Economy. Yale University Press.
Tirole, J. (2011). Illiquidity and all its friends. Journal of Economic Literature 49 (2), 287–325.

CHAPTER 7

Conclusions

Abstract This short monograph reviews the basic economic principles through which to look at the essence of recent blockchain-based monetary innovations and their implications, beginning with the different ways of trust that economists and computer scientists and meant to address. It is an educated guess that users of cryptocurrencies and stablecoins shall self-select their own ecologic niches, in connection with the expected forthcoming regulations. Arguing about the sense of a central bank digital currency (CBDC) is a more sophisticated endeavor that concerns in the first instance the foreseeable reverberations on the delicate equilibria along the hierarchy of account-based money. Beyond the efficiency and financial inclusion that motivate the CBDC construct, one notices that systemic central banks like the Fed or the ECB cannot afford to lag behind the technological frontier. The tension between the different methodologies employed by economists and computer scientists may prove useful in the ongoing inquiry about the potential of blockchain solutions.

Keywords Trust · Ecologic Niche · Hierarchy of Account-Based Money · Methodology

A. Schianchi and A. Mantovi, *The Economics of Cryptocurrencies and Digital Money*, Palgrave Studies in Financial Services Technology,
https://doi.org/10.1007/978-3-031-44248-3_7

The rate of technological progress has been a major driver of social and economic development since the first industrial revolution. Over the last decades, Information and Communication Technology (ICT) has had the pervasive impact that we experience in everyday life; blockchain and Fintech innovations represent an ongoing chapter of the tale. The blockchain has been envisioned as a general purpose technology, still, to date, its financial developments in terms of digital cash and smart contracts are what raise most of the interest of investors and media. The crypto downfall of fall 2022 has further increased our interest in the phenomenon.

In recent years an avalanche of new digital tokens has crowded the financial arena, and researchers and policymakers are required to cover the evolving landscape. Our journey has covered the basic economics of the phenomenon according to a philosophy that we summarize in this final chapter. We had no ambition to exhaust the economics of blockchain, nor to provide a satisfactory account of the crypto wave in terms of tokens, platforms, and characters (we refer to Prasad, 2021, for a beautiful account). The computer science of decentralized consensus characterizes the blockchain revolution, but we have devoted the least space to sketch its essentials. Shared ledgers and distributed record-keeping are no novelty, and the genuine innovation introduced by Nakamoto is the game theoretic dimension. This is the incipit of our philosophy.

Our approach builds on the premise that blockchain solutions and monetary institutions are meant to address different problems of trust. We have seen in Chapter 2 in which sense the blockchain construct aims at circumventing the need for a trustworthy central authority for the authentication of digital records. This kind of trust is localized at specific operations of nodes of the network, and is, so to say, backward looking, to the extent that it concerns the reliability of records of what transactions have already happened. Looking at the problem of time-stamping digital documents is perhaps the best way economists can approach the computer science of trust.

Monetary institutions face a different problem of trust, namely, a kind of trust that is inherently delocalized, in that it is a problem of network effects in sustaining decentralized beliefs about the acceptability of definite forms of money. In addition, the problem is forward looking, in that it concerns beliefs about what will happen (whether the acceptability of the means of exchange will maintain its role or not). Thus, at stake is not only correct record-keeping and authentication but also, most prominently, the institutional support to the liquidity and acceptability of money instruments. Central authorities (the central banks) coordinate such network effects and provide a public good that no blockchain can rival. The landmark model of bank runs developed by Diamond and Dybvig, which we have reviewed in Chapter 2, provides invaluable insights on the inherently network-strategic dimension of trust in monetary phenomena.

These basic insights underlie the development of our work. Game theory is the natural toolkit for the analysis of the Nakamoto design, which builds on Proof-of-Work. In the first part of the monograph we have developed the theme in terms of a basic game first, and then in terms of a number of more elaborate games. One can envision a hierarchy of complexity, in which a basic game form represents the fundamental degrees of freedom—the global hashrate and the differentiated cost competitiveness of players—of mining. Building on such a basic analytical setting, one develops more elaborate game forms admitting emergent phenomena as strategic equilibria. In this effort, we have been emphasizing the "instrumental" nature of the game theoretic approach.

We have represented the emergence of centralization in mining and in the vertical structure of the industry. This is in the first instance a theoretical problem, i.e. a problem of discussing the consistency itself of the Nakamoto design. To what extent the centralization of mining activity can be considered to undermine the philosophy of decentralized consensus? This is among the key questions that the nascent economics of cryptocurrencies is meant to address. Consequentially, the applied economic problem of centralization unfolds with a logic for looking at empirical patterns in terms of cogent degrees of freedom, like the strategic variables involved in the interaction between pools and miners.

In the second part of the monograph, we have been addressing the monetary dimension of the phenomenon. We have introduced the principle of "no questions asked" as the foundation of monetary economics, and the problem of safe assets as the monetary problem of the 2020s. In this perspective, the problem of stablecoins is much more than a problem of proper collateralization, and rather concerns the soundness of the concrete network in which these coins are meant to circulate, starting with issuers. In addition, we have seen in which sense the construct of a central bank digital currency is a delicate problem of the design of a future monetary system that may preserve the lessons learned from the great financial crisis. This is the philosophy that we have been unfolding through the chapters.

The Bitcoin protocol tailors a competition among miners that can be described as a Tullock contest. The game has been thoroughly investigated since the 1980s, with due emphasis on the linear aggregation property (responses can be represented as responses to the overall scale of activity). In recent years the unique Nash equilibrium of the game has been reconsidered in its implications for, on the one hand, the (theoretically fundamental) competition among risk-neutral unconstrained miners and, on the other hand, the (empirically relevant) competition between risk-averse miners and rational players in general. The former aspects have been the subject of Chapter 3, in which the discussions by Arnosti and Weinberg and Mantovi fix the basic building blocks of analysis—in particular, a number of original plots provide intuitive backing for analytic arguments concerning competitive advantages, entry thresholds and the complete pattern of best responses. The latter aspects have been the subject of Chapter 4, in which a number of model games of the recent literature have been sketched as generators of insights and interpretations of reality, for instance concerning the emergent concentration in mining.

Recall, Arnosti and Weinberg argue that risk-neutral mining is a natural oligopoly, and that such an outcome counters the inspiration itself of the Nakamoto philosophy. On the other hand, other researchers argue that decentralization is not really compromised and that mining pools emerge for risk sharing purposes, and spark market forces that counter overconcentration. One should not look for contradiction between these statements and rather appreciate the different degrees of freedom involved. Our methodologic digressions on instrumental game theory and backward induction were meant to sharpen the sense of our work, which we summarize as follows.

Social sciences in general, and economics in particular, deal with emergent phenomena that can hardly be represented as solutions to well-specified dynamical equations. Social phenomena emerge from a complex reality as *regularities* that can be discussed in analytic terms to some extent, but whose salient features are inherently qualitative (think of the great simplification embodied by the Solow model of economic growth). Simplicity is a plus in this setting. Simplicity is the opposite of naivety; simplicity is about the representation of an economic problem in the sharpest form. In this sense, economic modeling has been conceived as an *art*. One can think of the prisoners dilemma and of Akerlof lemons as examples of simple and far-reaching economic models whose logic can be communicated neatly. This is the type of discussion that we have targeted in our exposition.

It has been said that Bitcoin has failed to deliver on its promises, but some argue that perhaps its creator(s) had less ambition than the enthusiasts dreaming of a universal cryptocurrency that could substitute standard payment systems. It has been said that the plethora of tokens that followed Bitcoin was meant to fix its shortcomings, but simple intuition suggests that when an ecologic niche opens, soon it gets colonized. For sure, the phenomenon is in rapid evolution, and it matters to sharpen its monetary essence.

The coins generated by means of a blockchain protocol have no recognizable economic fundamentals. They are accepted in their own ecology that emerges as a self-selection of participants, much like Bitcoin miners are self-appointed. The fact that such tokens have turned into an asset class reflects the explosive interest in novelty, a form of (some may say irrational) exuberance that is not new to the history of finance. Exchanges of such tokens have grown rapidly in the absence of systematic regulation, and the crypto downfall of fall 2022 witnesses the criticality of the phenomenon, which has much in common with previous episodes of financial instability. In such respects, it matters to recall the relevance of what stands at the foundations of liquidity and acceptability.

Decentralized consensus does not support "money" in the same sense in which the balance sheet policy of a central bank supports a national currency. One such currency is universally accepted at par along the hierarchy of monetary institutions, with the central bank at the top that issues the monetary base, commercial banks just below that issue (the much larger stock of) bank money, and the subsequent tree of heterogeneous dealers issuing instruments (like MMMF shares) that display definite money attributes. Along the hierarchy, the problem of liquidity backstop has been adequately reconsidered in the wake of the great financial crisis, and the principle of NQA has been acknowledged as the fundamental property of money, the principle underlying the standard triple of textbook properties (store of value, means of exchange, and unit of account). Money is meant to be *safe* in the first instance.

The wide fluctuations in the value of cryptocurrencies are hardly compatible with such properties. Stablecoins have been conceived to fix this problem, as pegged to an international currency, typically the US dollar. This goal is achieved by backing the value of a stablecoin with suitable assets. This is in fact the mechanism in place along the hierarchy of money. Stablecoins as digital tokens are new from the technological point of view, but not from the monetary point of view of privately produced money. The analogy with MMMFs has been pointed out, as well as the fact that stablecoins issuers face the same problem that all banks inherently have.

Digital payments are already available in various forms, so why should one resort to stablecoins? The point revolves around the digital services and prices offered. Stablecoins may have a convenience yield associated with the specific technological services provided, but one must not forget that there is a lot of liquidity that is simply in search of parking space. This liquidity generated the advent of petrodollars and Eurodollars in the 1960s and of MMMF in the late 1970s. Thus, arguably, there may be substantial wholesale demand for stablecoins. There are somewhat established macroeconomic forces underlying the emergence of cash pools in search of parking space, namely, the financial reflection of real economy imbalances like excess global saving and the rising share of corporate profits relative to wages, and one may add the receipts of organized crime.

Thus we close the circle. Decentralized consensus was meant to circumvent the centralized management of money, but cryptocurrencies display wide fluctuations in value, and stablecoins are introduced to stem such fluctuations, which plague the transition from the exchange function to the store of value function of cryptocurrencies. Stablecoins need to be backed by safe assets, and here we come full circle. We come back to the hierarchy of account-based money, in which any form of money is a liability backed by the left-hand side of a balance sheet.

In particular, stablecoin issuers face a subtle tradeoff that marks recent advances in the understanding of financial stability. On the one hand, the issuer of a stablecoin wants the public to trust the properness of the collateralization adopted. The issuer has therefore incentives to disclose information about the quality of the assets that back the value of the coin. On the other hand, transparency comes at the cost of information sensitivity, which may result in emerging panic and potential runs on the coin. Therefore, the same issuer may want to maintain opacity and information insensitivity on the collateralization of the coin. This tradeoff is not specific to stablecoins, and impinges virtually on every financial intermediary (one may dare say on any firm), and still, standard textbooks do not seem to acknowledge the fundamental status of this insight. It is here where the problem of the regulation of stablecoins displays its relevance in full bloom, as discussed by Gorton and Zhang.

Then one comes to central banks as regulators and policymakers, Major central banks are hovering around the plan to start CBDCs. In some cases, the experiment is already at an advanced stadium. Bitter criticism has been raised against the CBDC construct, which has been depicted as a solution in search of a problem, and as a tentative answer to an ill-posed question. For sure, major central banks cannot afford to lag behind the technological frontier. The future is open for us to see. It is arguable that cryptocurrencies and stablecoins will select their own niches both as payment systems and asset class. It may be worth noticing that the classical economics of portfolio theory may find interesting challenges in assessing the riskiness of cryptocurrencies in a frequentist approach, and a Bayesian framework may provide enlightening insights on the problem.

We have seen in Chapter 6 that the debate on the regulation of cryptocurrencies ranges between polar ideas. At one extreme, one advocates minimal regulation; what really matters is to make the public aware of the inherent uncertainties involved. At another extreme, one advocates comprehensive regulation, since it matters for society to avoid the systemic risks generated by potential shocks in a crypto environment, which may spill over onto the rest of the financial system. Such polar ideas should be properly combined in the policy and regulation design to come. It is not so clear, at least to us, how to balance the relative importance of regulating cryptocurrencies as a means of exchange on a private (partially regulated?) platform and as assets traded in a (comprehensively regulated) network of dealers. We have pointed out that the recent turmoil pertains to the latter dimension, and that it has been a questionable practice to promote cryptocurrencies to an asset class just because there has been substantial demand for it. At the time of writing (spring 2023) the elucidation of the details of the crack FTX is ongoing, and such details will be useful for thinking about the specificities of the problems we are debating.

In recent years a number of researchers have been emphasizing that securities do not live in empty space, and rather inhabit specific balance sheets of dealers that, in turn, do not operate in a vacuum, and rather inhabit definite networks of intermediaries. Such a vision represents a line of development of financial economics according to which an asset class is a concept whose consistency is a function, among other things, of the soundness of the concrete network of dealers in which it is traded. The liquidity of an asset is an *emergent* phenomenon, not an intrinsic property of a security that carries claims on some fundamentals.

The debate on the desirability of CBDC is somewhat narrower. No enthusiasts and no light-hearted spirit. Virtually every commentator has been arguing that central banks should be prudent in the design of CBDC, and some of them state explicitly that central banks should avoid the enterprise. In our view, the debate should be framed with respect to the hierarchy of institutions that issue the hierarchy of money. Having public access to the balance sheet of the central bank ("reserves for all") induces a short circuit in the hierarchy of money, whose consequences may be partly foreseeable (like the partial displacement of commercial banks) and partly involve unknown unknowns. For instance, Gorton and Zhang argue about the potential consequences of the expansion of the balance sheet of the central bank. Accepting accounts implies buying something and thereby enlarging the balance sheet in some direction, with potential distortions in capital markets. The central bank may turn out in effect to pursue some form of fiscal policy.

This rapid evolution of events is adequately accounted for by specialized media, and a monograph aiming at a comprehensive account of what has already happened would be not only voluminous but also rapidly out of date. This brief monograph is meant to provide elements for looking at events (both past and future) with a clear economic logic. The ongoing analytical developments on aggregative games may provide further hints. Over the last decades, researchers have renewed interest in contests as a fundamental economic approach *complementary* to the general equilibrium picture. Our focus on aggregative games and in-and-out-of-equilibrium best responses may therefore display general implications beyond the specific application to PoW.

Economists and computer scientists, in a sense, move in opposite directions. Economics aims at simplified pictures of regularities that emerge from complex social phenomena that cannot be represented in a complete model, and that are not replicable. Computer science, on the other hand, aims at sharpening the description of systems that, in principle, can be represented by complete models, and that can be replicated at will. This logical tension may prove beneficial in the theoretical inquiry on the potential of blockchain solutions.

Index

A. Schianchi and A. Mantovi, *The Economics of Cryptocurrencies and Digital Money*, Palgrave Studies in Financial Services Technology,
https://doi.org/10.1007/978-3-031-44248-3